Thi

MW00906363

is a gift to:

_____

From:

_____

On:

_____

Dedications

To my family who supports me; to Helen Nichols, a teacher who continually challenged me to "do better"; to Frances Burnside, a librarian who listened to everything I wrote and introduced me to *The Writer* when I was nine years old; and to Mabel Mathias, who made it possible for me to obtain my first writing job.

Donna Goodrich

In appreciation to my helpful husband, Howard, and my dear writer/speaker friends who generously shared their talents with us.

Mary Lou Klingler

To my husband, Rick, for his patience in computer instruction and help with late-night manuscript polishing! Also a special thanks to my friend, Lou Goodgame, whose continued encouragement inspired this book.

Jan Potter

Acknowledgments

A special thanks to our typist, Marsha Crockett, and our calligraphers, Lauren Knowles, Leigh Knowles, and Betsy Nunley.

100 ^{Plus}

Motivational Moments
for
Writers and Speakers

Compiled and Edited
by
Donna Goodrich, Mary Lou Klingler,
and Jan Potter

JOY PUBLISHING
PO Box 827
San Juan Capistrano, California

Bible Versions Quoted:

KJV - King James Version
NIV - From the Holy Bible, New International Version. © 1973,1978,1984
International Bible Society. Used by permission of Zondervan Bible Publishers.
NAB - New American Bible ©1970 by the Confraternity of Christian Doctrine,
Wahington D.C.
NASB - Scripture taken fron the New American Standard Bible, © 1960, 1962,
1963, 1968, 1971, 1972, 1973, 1975, 1977 by The Lockman Foundation. Used by
permission.
RSV - From the Revised Standard Version of the Bible, copyrighted 1946 and 1952
by the Division of Christian Education of the NCCC, U.S.A
TLB - Scripture verses are taken from The Living Bible © 1971 owned by
assignment by Illinois Regional Bank N.A. (as trustee). Used by permission of
Tyndale House Publishers, Inc., Wheaton, IL 60189. All rights reserved.
AMP - From *The Amplified Bible*. Old Testament copyright © 1965, 1987 by The
Zondervan Corporation. The Amplified New Testament copyright © 1958, 1987 by
The Lockman Foundation. Used by permission.
NKJV - From the *New King James Version*. Copyright © 1979, 1980, 1982, Thomas
Nelson Inc., Publishers. Used by permission.
TEV - From the *Good News Bible* — Old Testament: Copyright © American Bible
Society 1976;New Testament;Copyright ©American Bible Society 1966, 1971, 1976.
NEB - The New English Bible ©The Delegates of the Oxford University Press and
the Syndics of the Cambridge University Press 1961, 1970

Copyright 1991 by Joy Publishing
All rights reserved
No portion of this book may be copied or reprinted without the
express permission of Joy Publishing, San Juan Capistrano,
California, with the exception of a review of this book whereby
brief passages may be quoted by the reviewer with proper credit
line. Write for permission to the address below.

Printed by Princeton University Press
Library of Congress Cataloging-in-Publication data

100 Plus Motivational Moments for Writers and Speakers
Compiled by Donna Goodrich, Mary Lou Klingler, and Jan Potter
1.Writers/Speakers — devotionals 2. Goodrich, Donna
3. Klingler, Mary Lou 4. Potter, Jan 5. Devotional - Biblical
meditations
CIP # 91-62088
International Standard Book Number 0-939513-45-5

Joy Publishing
P.O. Box 827
San Juan Capistrano CA 92675

Table of Contents

Preface

Behind every book lies a story. This book is no exception. I share this story with you that you may find encouragement in the visions and ideas the Lord has given **you**.

In 1984, in two separate cities, in two different states, the Lord touched four hearts with a compelling drive to tend to the needs of Christian writers.

Three of the four individuals knew each other, as they were all part of a critique group that met in the Phoenix, Arizona area. The members of the trio expressed to each other concern about the lack of appropriate devotional books written for writers. They decided to take leadership in bringing together authors who could produce such a book.

They were so encouraged by the positive response they received when they shared their idea with other writers that they developed a book proposal and mailed it to a publisher.

While waiting to hear word from the publisher, they continued to write their own devotionals and to ask others to join them in their effort. So many of the devotionals they received came with prayers that God would bless their efforts.

After what felt like forever, a letter arrived from the publisher. It said that while the idea was great, the market was too narrow and therefore could not be pursued by that company.

Undaunted, the trio prayed for guidance and then sent the proposal to another publisher. The second "official" response to the proposal carried the same message as the first: Great idea — market too narrow.

Years passed as more letters were sent, covered in prayer, and more were received, full of rejection. Then, after twenty-three attempts to find a publisher, I, the fourth person of the group, caught a glimpse of the Lord's plan for the book.

The Lord often creates out of nothing what He needs to accomplish His will. Joy Publishing is a good example of this process.

In January of 1984, I was a non-writer, without any thoughts of publishing. Suddenly, a series of unplanned and unexpected events occurred that resulted in my first book being published in June of that year. Out-of-the-ordinary events continued. By the fall of 1986, Joy Publishing was established to handle my own publications and to explore joint projects with other writers. Over the next two years a special ministry of assistance to Christian writers and speakers developed and I felt myself being called to address the needs of a market that other publishers had dismissed as too narrow to be worth their time.

Joy Publishing and its subsequent success truly was the Lord's doing — a case of creating something out of nothing in order to accomplish His purpose. I am currently working on a book which will tell the whole story in greater detail.

I met the first three members of the group at the 1990 Phoenix Writers Conference. Within six months after our meeting this book was ready to go to press. What had begun years before as a desire to meet Christian writer's needs had finally turned into reality.

The message that I want to leave with you from this story is this: God **does** answer prayer. All things **do** work together for good to those who love God and who are called according to His purposes. It just happens according to His timetable, not ours. He created something out of nothing, a whole publishing company, just to get this book into your hands. Imagine what He will do in response to **your** prayers!

Woody Young
Publisher

Introduction

Before you begin to write your article or speech, take a moment for meditation. Where do others get their inspiration? How do they determine priorities? How do they overcome the desire to sharpen pencils or chat with friends when they should be punching the keyboard?

At last, a book of scriptural encouragement and exhortation for the Christian writer, speaker, pastor, teacher, or anyone who prepares messages for others.

Following each devotional, we've included the start of a prayer to help you reflect on what you've read. Please write your thoughts in the space provided: it will greatly enhance the benefit you receive from this book.

We pray that this book will motivate you to use your talents and view your craft as a calling from the God Who deserves your best effort.

Donna Goodrich, Mary Lou Klingler, and Jan Potter

My command is this ~
Love each other
as I have loved YOU.
Greater love has
no one than this,
that one lay down
his life
for his FRIENDS...

Lauren Knowles

John 15:12-14

FEED MY SHEEP

Floyd Allen

Simon, son of Jonas, lovest thou me?...Feed my sheep.
(John 21:15, KJV)

As Christian writers, we must believe that our calling is more than a subtle suggestion of some distant muse, more than just a self-gratifying whim. It is the means by which many hearts will be touched.

Often I find myself falling victim to the temptation not to write. As the flow of my creative juices ebbs and I slip into less-than-acceptable writing habits, the Holy Spirit quickens the above verse to me and I know that I must re-establish my priorities and put pen to paper. In this chapter, Jesus asks Peter three times if he loves Him and, when assured that he does, Jesus admonishes him to "feed my sheep."

As both an author and an educator, I accept that through me Jesus can touch others. Even though at times I feel I just cannot go on, I know that -- because I love Him -- I, too, must "feed the sheep."

13

God is my Enabler !!

Lord, You know I love You. You have asked me to feed Your sheep, therefore …

I will renew my vow to write something every day – even if I only have time for a journal entry. I praise you, Lord, for my first article to be published (Our Sunday Visitor "Have You Kissed A Frog Today?" – 2/21/93). I pray the words which you have given me to write will touch the lives of those whom you will to read them, and that your name be exalted + praised – for your honor & glory.

An author of a novel entitled *The Ananias Precedent* and many short stories, **Floyd Allen** is an educator at Northwest Christian Academy and Western Bible Institute in Phoenix, Arizona. He has also spoken to writers' groups and taught at conferences.

COMMITMENT TO EXCELLENCE

Margaret J. Anderson

Commit thy works unto the Lord, and thy thoughts shall be established. (Proverbs 16:3, KJV)

One evening I sat altering the neckline of a sale-purchased dress. Defying repeated manipulation, one side gapped unmanageably. I must have sighed or in some way expressed my exasperation for, without warning, my husband spoke.

"Why be so fussy?" he asked. "It looks okay to me."

I flashed him one of my "oh-come-now" looks which meant, "You ought to know me better than that."

He understood. Chuckling, he said, "Okay, have it your way. By this time I should know you won't give up until you are satisfied it fits perfectly."

So it is with writing. We must not give up until our words fit as perfectly as we can make them.

Writing takes a commitment to excellence with a strong belief in what we are doing. We have the power, in our words, to change people's lives. We must feel the urgency of His schedule. If we're speaking, writing or even sewing, we should do it as unto the Lord.

The person who commits his/her time whole-heartedly to Christ's guidance and instruction will never be the same again, either. Always there will be an achievement goal, a never-satisfied urge to be the best for Him.

Lord, with Your help, I'm ready to …

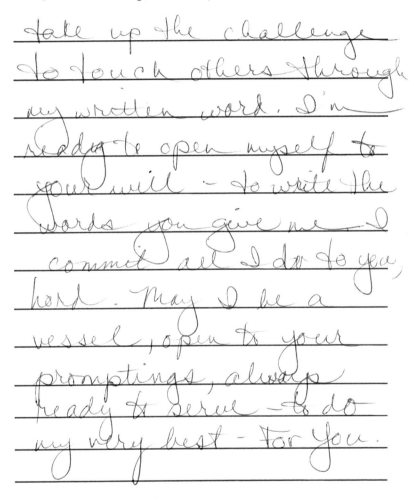

take up the challenge to touch others through my written word. I'm ready to open myself to your will – to write the words you give me. I commit all I do to you, Lord. May I be a vessel, open to your promptings, always ready to serve – to do my very best – for you.

Margaret J. Anderson lives in Turlock, California. She has published 19 books, including *The Christian Writer's Handbook*, which has gained much acclaim in the writing world. She has also been a writing instructor at almost 60 workshops and conferences.

THE OPPORTUNITY TO GIVE

Mary W. Anderson

It is more blessed to give than to receive.
(Acts 20:35, KJV)

After my cousin Guelda retired, I kept in touch by occasional letters but never expected a response. In the fall of 1990, a relative called to say that Guelda had terminal cancer. She said Guelda enjoyed my letters and wanted me to continue writing.

Sometimes while writing an article for publication, God would interrupt my train of thought and remind me of the opportunity to give. I was pushed to write Guelda, or a former recently-widowed co-worker who had moved away. Later I wrote another friend with a severe respiratory problem who lost his wife and only sister, and I write to an asthmatic friend who lives alone in an isolated area and grieves for her murdered grandchild.

But now Guelda needed more support. So I telephoned to ask if I could refer her to the church prayer line. I knew the members would also send cards and notes. She replied, "Yes, please do. I need all the prayers I can get."

During the period when Guelda faced death, I wrote

17

her six days a week. She loved stories about her aunts and grandfather and her mother's early life. Sometimes I included photos and clippings. My upbeat letters expressed love and concern and said, "I care."

After three months, Guelda entered the hospital. While the family waited for the end, they read my letters. After Guelda's death, they told me how much the letters meant to all of them.

I had the opportunity to give and remembered what Jesus said, "It is more blessed to give than to receive."

Jesus, bless my giving to ...

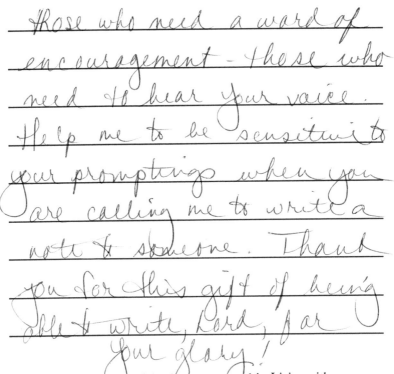

Those who need a word of encouragement - those who need to hear your voice. Help me to be sensitive to your promptings when you are calling me to write a note to someone. Thank you for this gift of being able to write, Lord, for your glory!

Mary W. Anderson's articles have appeared in *Living with Teenagers, Mature Years, Arizona Senior World,* and the *Las Vegas Review-Journal.* She lives in Tempe, Arizona.

WHEN IT'S NOT EASY

Marlene Bagnull

Let us fix our eyes on Jesus, the author and perfecter of our faith. (Hebrews 12:2, NIV)

"Lord, why is it so hard?" I have asked many times. I may be laboring to fill a blank sheet of paper with words for an assignment that is due. Or I may have just opened the day's mail and found only printed rejection forms from editors who normally purchase my work. Or, most difficult of all, the book I felt called to write may have just been returned for the twenty-first time.

"There must be an easier way to serve you," I complain to the Lord. But then I am chastened by my word choice.

Easy? It wasn't easy for Jesus to experience hostility, criticism and rejection from the people who had been praying for Him to come. It wasn't easy for Him to endure the physical, emotional, and spiritual pain of the cross. Isaiah tells how He was despised and rejected, "a man of sorrows, acquainted with bitterest grief." (53:3)

When I think of all Jesus suffered, my own struggles seem insignificant. I am reminded that He never promised it would be easy to follow Him, but He has promised always to be with me. The answer to discouragement comes through keeping my eyes on Him. Only then will I be enabled to discover the joy of service and sacrifice, and find the strength to "not grow weary and lose heart." (Hebrews 12:3)

Jesus, as I am strengthened by You, I can ...

_____

_____

_____

_____

_____

_____

_____

_____

Marlene Bagnull has made over 976 sales to 105 different Christian periodicals and is the author of three books including *Write His Answer--Encouragement for Christian Writers.* She is the founder and director of the Greater Philadelphia Christian Writers Fellowship and its annual conference. Marlene lives in Drexel Hill, Pennsylvania and has taught at many Christian writers' conferences.

WRITING CREATIVELY

Stanley C. Baldwin

*In the beginning God created the heaven and the earth...
And God created man in His own image.*
(Genesis 1:1,27a, NAS)

The first thing we read about God in the Bible is that He created the universe. And the first thing we read about man is that he bears God's image. This suggests that man is creative, too.

God alone can create in the sense of bringing something from nothing. Except for the first verse, however, the Genesis account describes another kind of creativity: bringing order and meaning to an existing earth that was formless, empty, and dark, God used available material to make new forms.

God made man, more than a million different species of animals, and over 300,000 different species of plants--all from the same basic dirt. Science tells us that all things--inanimate and living--are composed from only about 100 different elements.

The writer has a similar task--to create diverse new forms from a few basic components--26 letters. Writers select from the jumbled mass of over 750,000 words just the right ones and arrange them to create new works of order, beauty, and meaning.

At least, that's what we should do. Many forces conspire against our creativity, pressuring us to conform, to play it safe, to say the same old things in the same old ways.

The secret to resisting this temptation is in having the courage to be ourselves. God made each of us unique. If we will be ourselves, we'll be creatively different from everyone else.

Thank you, Lord, that I am fearfully and wonderfully made. Give me the freedom and courage to be my creative self.

Lord, my creative self, which you made unique unto me, has started ...

_____

_____

_____

_____

_____

_____

_____

_____

Stanley C. Baldwin has been writing for publication for over 26 years. He has authored 16 books and hundreds of articles and has taught Christian writers in America, Africa, and India. He makes his home in Oregon City, Oregon.

WRITE
NOW

Millie Barger

Jesus said, "Follow me." But he said, "Lord, first let me..."
(Luke 9:59, KJV)

"Someday, when I become a grandmother, then I'll write, Lord, I'll write for you. But first, let me..."

As a busy teenager, that seemed logical. Writing school assignments was enough, yet a budding desire to be a writer stirred within.

It sprouted again when as a young mother I hurriedly penned short programs for church and school. Busy with home, work, husband, and energetic children, logic again prevailed.

In my middle-age years, involvement in church work, community activities, hobbies, and babysitting grandchildren left me with no idle hours. NEVER did a block of time confront me demanding, "Write!" Again I parroted the procrastinator's logic of "someday."

Life accelerated. As a senior citizen I have numerous interests and still struggle to fulfill my lifelong dream of writing. Thinking back through the years of all the stories I could have written, of all the poems I might have penned, of all the ideas left to germinate in the darkness of my files, I deeply regret my procrastination.

Gradually, I have cleared the garden of my retirement years to allow patches of time. I unstop bottled creative waters and they moisten my unproductive gray matter. Warmed by the sun of God's approval, signs of new growth appear. However, it only happens each day as I tell myself, WRITE NOW!

Heavenly Father, "someday" has arrived. Today I will ...

_____

_____

_____

_____

_____

_____

_____

_____

_____

_____

_____

Millie Barger has published three drama books, hundreds of articles, and has three books in process. She is the co-leader of the Bethany Christian Writer's Club in Phoenix, Arizona, and teaches workshops on writing devotionals.

WHEN OPPORTUNITY KNOCKS

Marilyn Gwaltney Barnes

Be very careful, then, how you live -- not as unwise but as wise, making the most of every opportunity, because the days are evil. (Ephesians 5:15,16, NIV)

As an author and a staff member of Campus Crusade for Christ, I'm often asked to speak at various functions -- Mothers of Preschoolers (MOPS) meetings, mother-daughter banquets, or church women's retreats. Because I am also a wife and mother of three active school-age children, I find that I need to evaluate each speaking opportunity in light of my own goals and objectives, since my time for outside ministry is limited.

Some time ago I realized that quite often I was asked to speak on topics that had little spiritual impact. I decided that since my time was precious, I wanted to make every speaking opportunity count for eternity.

Now whenever I'm asked to address a group of women, I tailor my message to fit one of three general areas: evangelism, prayer and the ministry of the Holy Spirit, or the Great Commission. Why? Because I've found that most people fall into one of those three categories. If they are not Christians, they need to know Jesus as Savior and Lord. If they are Christians,

25

either they need to understand how to pray and walk in the power of God's Spirit, or they should be challenged to take Christ's Great Commission seriously.

These guidelines help me to wisely determine whether or not to accept a particular speaking request. Usually when I explain my priorities, the women are eager to have me speak on one of these three topics. Since the days truly are evil, I want to make the most of my time and the opportunities God brings my way.

Lord, I ask that You continue to fill me with the Holy Spirit that I might ...

_____

_____

_____

_____

_____

_____

_____

_____

Marilyn Barnes, of Littleton, Colorado, is the author of one book, *Love (and Baby Powder) Covers All*, a devotional for young mothers, and writes a monthly column for the Denver Christian News. She has also been published in many periodicals and is a speaker at MOPS groups, church functions, and retreats throughout Colorado.

AN INSTRUMENT

Virginia Perez Benton

He that believeth on me, as the scripture hath said, out of his belly shall flow rivers of living water. (John 7:38, KJV)

I once had the privilege of co-pastoring a small home missions church. At one particular worship service, the mood was reverent and whispers of adoration could be heard.

Then someone began to sing softly a song that asks God to make us instruments for His use. I was especially moved by the lyrics and at that moment, I felt quite "spiritual." Loftily, I imagined myself to be a beautiful shiny trumpet of extraordinary quality.

Quicker than I had imagined myself such a fine instrument, God opened my spiritual eyes and I saw a water pitcher of coarse metal and little worth. It was dull gray with a belly of distended roundness and a wide--almost flat-- lip. It was by far the most graceless spout I had ever seen, and it distressed me to see it.

I considered the contrast of the instruments and could have laughed at my childish envisioning of myself, if I hadn't been so embarrassed by my pomp. Yet, I barely had time to repent of my pride before the Lord showed me an overflowing of water continuously pouring out from this most homely but serviceable pitcher.

This experience taught me I cannot improve upon any gift of grace by imagining it to be other than it is. I also learned that refinement of ability comes by practicing the use of a gift to the fullest.

Assured that God will not leave me too long in the shallowness of indulging pride, I can enthusiastically urge others: to practice that which motivates and is a heart's desire for service, to speak and share experiences that inspire others, to put godly thoughts in writing, and to be an encourager. By virtue of practice, God will enhance.

God, You know the refinement I need. Guide me to practice my ...

_____

_____

_____

_____

_____

_____

_____

_____

Virginia Perez Benton has spoken at many churches and has addressed small and large groups such as Aglow Fellowship. She lives in Chandler, Arizona.

THE VISION

Darlene Bogle

*For the vision is yet for an appointed time, but at the end
it shall speak, and not lie; though it tarry, wait for it,
because it will surely come, it will not tarry.*

(Habakkuk 2:3, KJV)

Six years had passed since my vision had first gained
clarity in my heart. I had moved from wanting to be a
writer to knowing that I was to write a book. It would
not only educate and encourage the Christian
community with a message of hope for the homosexual,
but would send a shaft of light into the darkness of the
homosexual world itself.

Six years--and six rewrites later, I mailed yet another
manuscript copy to a publisher. I'd been through the
process before--and received nine rejections, although
they thought the manuscript was "well written."

It was "too controversial" and if only I'd "remove
certain portions from the manuscript," two publishers
said they would be very interested in publishing my
material.

I would have to compromise my presentation of the
truth as I'd lived it, just to reach a market. I toyed with
the idea. "Could I live with publication at any cost?"

"I can't compromise what I believe," I told a writing
friend. "Even if it means that I sell this book a chapter
at a time."

"Read Habakkuk 2:3, Darlene," she responded, "and

be patient."

Instead of reaching for my modern translation of the Bible, I removed my worn King James from the shelf and opened it to the reference. A notation entered almost twenty years earlier almost leapt off the page: "Someday I'll write a book!" A faded arrow pointed to verse three.

I sighed, and entered a new comment: "Re-confirmed, March 1984."

Within the week, a publisher called wanting to publish my manuscript. The long-awaited contract was in the mail.

While I could have compromised principles and deleted some material to have my book published, I realized God's vision is much better than mine. His appointed time was not to be swayed by my impatience and while I waited, I learned a more important lesson: It was the life I lived, not the words I wrote that really mattered.

Lord, help me re-confirm my commitment to ...

Darlene Bogle lives in Hayward, California and is the author of three books, *Daughter, Are You Listening?*, a daily devotional for women; and two books offering hope and healing for the homosexual: *Long Road to Love* and *Strangers in a Christian Land*. She has also contributed to two other books. She is a licensed minister, a speaker and teacher at Christian writers conferences, and the Director of Paraklete Ministries, an outreach to the homosexual.

And let us not lose heart in doing good, for in due time we shall reap if we do not grow weary.

GALATIANS 6:9

btpd©

COMMITMENT

*Commit your works to the Lord, and your plans will be
established.*   (Proverbs 16:3, NAS)

When writing devotional material, I commit my
work plans to the Lord, then writing indeed becomes
nourishment for the soul. I cannot help but feel God's
power inspiring me, when I ask His help in releasing my
creative energy. As threads of an idea drift into my
mind, I type them out, not concerned at the time with
special form or sequence of material.

Closing my eyes sometimes helps capture an elusive
mental image. I feel relaxed, as I allow my thoughts to
materialize. Seeing my expression on paper, I am then
encouraged to expand the idea--one thread adheres to
another, until a tapestry of words is woven. Revision,
form, etc., come much later.

When satisfied that I have presented my best work,
I type the final draft. It is then I pray: "Lord, I accept
this work as Thy will for me to express something which
might be of help to others--to give encouragement, joy,
or love."

I also pray to write not for selfish ambition, nor to
use deceiving words, but to write so that God will say
"well done" when my work is finished. Have I said all
that He would have me say, in the right manner? In my
heart I feel I know the answer. My pledge is that I will
always try to submit material pleasing to God. I thank
Him, and feel humble to be chosen one of his "bearers
of good news." The world needs more Christian writers.

Jesus, I pray that with Your help my creative energy will...

_____

_____

_____

_____

_____

_____

_____

_____

_____

_____

_____

_____

_____

Sara Brandon lives in Phoenix, Arizona and is the author of many articles and poems. She was a regular contributor to a column in the *Arizona Republic*. Sara has also self-published family histories, two books of poetry, and several books of short stories.

A TIME FOR EVERYTHING

Gina Bridgeman

To everything there is a season, and a time to every purpose under the heaven...a time to keep silence, and a time to speak. (Ecclesiastes 3:1,7b, KJV)

I walked in the house and tossed the mail on the kitchen table.

"I'm so discouraged," I said to my husband Paul. The latest issue of a national inspirational magazine had just arrived, highlighting a friend's article, her fourth in as many months.

"I haven't even submitted anything to them in over a year," I sighed.

"Your time will come," Paul said, but his words offered little comfort. You see, most of my writing time has been stolen by a small wonder...a baby. I'm a full-time mother, trying to write in what time I can steal back or find left over each day. But the fatigue and the unpredictable demands of keeping a home and family running smoothly often pre-empt my best intentions to spend the afternoon at the word processor.

How can I use the gifts God gave me? I ask in frustration. Answering me are the above words of Ecclesiastes, a gentle reminder that God has given me

35

many gifts as well as the proper time for using all of them. Right now, being a mother is most important, and sometimes the accompanying duties--taking my energetic little boy to the park on a warm spring day, sitting quietly with him when he doesn't feel well, or spending an hour rearranging the closet to keep his busy little fingers out of trouble--must come first. And it's all right when those things temporarily keep me from writing. That time I "keep silence" is preparation time, the "time to plant" until the harvesting of ideas comes and it's time to write.

I try to make the most of those hours, finding ideas in our daily activities, letting them settle in my mind and germinate, taking quick notes, and journal writing every day, if only for five minutes. The result? A devotional idea at the park, a column idea from a family dinner table conversation, an article idea while watching other young mothers at the shopping mall. In my life, God has made a time for everything. It's my job to enjoy today's time, all the while preparing for tomorrow's.

Heavenly Father, please show me how I can show my love today by ...

_____

_____

_____

Gina Bridgeman's work has appeared in several inspirational magazines including Guideposts and Standard. She is a regular contributor to the annual devotional book Daily Guideposts. Gina also co-authored the book, *It's Anybody's Ballgame*, with her dad, Joe Garagiola, former major league baseball player and announcer. She resides in Scottsdale, Arizona.

THE PRINCIPLE WORKS

Jean Bryant

*I will wash mine hands in innocency: so will I compass
thine altar, O Lord: that I may publish with the voice of
thanksgiving, and tell of all thy wondrous works.*

(Psalm 26:6-7, KJV)

Is this writing game really worthwhile? Does my
writing make a difference to anyone? How can I be
assured of success?

Those questions continually poked at my mind when
I first became serious about the writing business. It was
a big step for me--I was past fifty, and more than a little
frightened.

Long believing that God's Word held answers, and
wanting to get started right, I looked up "publish" in my
concordance. The above verse is what I found.

There was my answer. I would have to admit the
sins in my life, face them, confess them, and then leave
them. The forgiveness and cleansing promised in I
John 1:9 would provide me with the innocency needed
to qualify for approaching the altar of God. Then, as a
result of my meeting with Him, I knew I could be
thankful for whatever I wrote and published, and
realized that even I could presume to tell of all His

wondrous works.

So we started on that basis, just God and me. It wasn't easy for me because I had quite an accumulation of sins to face, both large and small. However, the principle worked! I recognized it clearly one day when I was so overwhelmed with wonder at what God had done through me, my breath caught and then let go in a splash of tears.

That was several years ago. Now as the managing editor of a publishing company, I find this principle still holds. I know because I have to use it often. The books we publish tell of God's wondrous works, and I experience success and can speak with thanksgiving in my voice when I stay right with God, when I get the sins taken care of by washing "mine hands in innocency."

Dear Lord, I confess ...

_____

_____

_____

_____

_____

_____

_____

Jean Bryant is the Managing Editor of Here's Life Publishers in San Bernadino, California. She teaches editing at numerous writers conferences, and also published "Lois" magazine for two years.

TRUST HIM!

Bea Carlton

Trust in the Lord with all thine heart, and lean not unto thine own understanding. (Proverbs 3:5, KJV)

I claim this promise from God for my writing and speaking ministries. I ask for inspiration; then I trust Him for it. Often I tell the Lord: "I'm your hand extended to these people."

Jesus is my computer expert. I was typing the final copy of a book when my printer refused to print. No one could tell me why the computer refused to obey the print command.

I was rapidly coming unglued! My husband urged me to calm down and to trust that God would help. I told the Lord I was trusting Him with it and went to bed. The next morning a thought slipped into my mind: Try a diskette that doesn't have the book's title on it. It printed without a hitch. Since then I've had to go to Him for His computer expertise several times.

After my first book manuscript was rejected several times, I got serious with the Lord and asked specifically where to send it. My answer was Accent Books. If I had known anything about Accent Books I wouldn't have sent it there. They had no romantic mystery category. They now have a romantic mystery line and I have sold them eight books. Trusting Him works!

Sometimes our beginning writing isn't good enough to sell, but we can trust Him to help us there, too. We must be willing to practice our craft, learning the perfecting. And He will give us peace of mind while He works out a path for us.

Holy Father, I'm entrusting ...

_____

_____

_____

_____

_____

_____

_____

_____

_____

_____

_____

Bea Carlton of Willcox, Arizona is the author of eight romance mystery novels published by Accent Publishers and a book on puppet ministries. She also teaches classes on novel writing at writers' conferences.

BE

STILL

Dan Carr

Be still, and know that I am God.
(Psalm 46:10, KJV)

I believe that part of the equipment built into every writer is the strong unending desire to get words on paper as rapidly as possible. There is a deep fear that to fail to do so is to fail as a writer. After all, isn't the job of the writer to write?

More and more I am convinced that God is drilling the words of the Psalmist into my thick skull. Be still! Be still! Stop and listen to the sounds around you! Hear the bird's song! Listen to the wind blowing through the trees! Feel it on your face. Experience the senses I have given you. Hear the words I have to say to you. Be still!

And "know that I am God." To "know" God is to know Him in an intimate personal relationship. To spend your entire life letting the One who loves you know you, and for the two of you to become so wrapped up in each other that it would be impossible to separate you.

Stillness and knowledge are two vital ingredients in the life of the writer. As we develop the ability to realize there is a time to write and a time not to write, and as we let God reveal Himself to us as He has done in Jesus Christ, we become not only better writers but more aware of God's presence in our lives.

And yes, there is a difference between "stillness" and procrastination.

My Lord and Savior, I promise to be ...

_____

_____

_____

_____

_____

_____

_____

_____

_____

_____

_____

Dan Carr is a minister and free-lance writer who lives in Bar Mills, Maine. He has written children's books, magazine articles, and over 200 greeting cards, and also leads a writer's group.

JOIN THE BATTLE

Charlotte Casey

And take the helmet of salvation, and the sword of the Spirit, which is the word of God. (Ephesians 6:17, RSV)

"I got it back with a polite rejection slip," our young minister told us. "I think they felt sorry for me."

The congregation had urged him to submit some of his sermons, always so original and timely, for publication. His disappointment and discouragement showed, in spite of his smile and joke about his writing.

I knew the feeling.

"Join the club," I told him. I should have said, "Join the battle," because Christian writers are fighting a spiritual battle and we can't afford to forget it.

Questions come like "Am I really good enough?" or "Am I kidding myself?" "Maybe I'd better quit wasting time and money and just forget the whole thing," we tell ourselves.

When these doubts bombard me, I tend to quit sending out manuscripts for a while, to retreat and lick my wounds. Then I can sneer at the mailbox, "Yah, yah, no rejects today!" as though I sure fixed those editors who don't recognize a masterpiece when I send them one.

It's then I realize that I'm allowing Satan to win by default. Persistence and patience come with the territory. Who am I, some prima donna who shouldn't have to pay her dues and sweat out some rejections?

God reminds us to "take the helmet of salvation" that guards our minds and keeps our thinking clear. We're to attack with the sharp sword of God's Word. No wonder Satan wants to shut us up!

So join the battle! We follow a great Commander-in-Chief -- the Lion of Judah. And we have an arsenal of words, powerful weapons, to tell of Him.

O Lord, grant me persistence to ...

_____

_____

_____

_____

_____

_____

_____

Charlotte Casey is a Bible teacher and former English and speech teacher. Her articles and poems have been published in the *Kent State Quarterly, the Arizona Republic, Desert Haven Community Church Lenten Devotionals, Decision*, and *A Time For Singing.* Charlotte lives in Tempe, Arizona.

WHOSE JOB IS THIS?

Karen L. Chole

Therefore, my beloved brethren, be steadfast, immovable, always abounding in the work of the Lord, knowing that your toil is not in vain in the Lord.

(1 Corinthians 15:58, NAS)

Reaching for my time management notebook, I scheduled in writing time for the coming week. If I stayed on target, I could squeeze in three hours of final revisions on my manuscript for the next four mornings. Under Friday I wrote "Herald Press--UPS" and said to myself, "Finally I will get rid of this book."

After I had worked for about an hour, the phone rang. I considered letting the answering machine take it, but curiosity got the best of me. Edith, a fellow writer, was calling to see how I was progressing. While I brought her up-to-date, I continued to make corrections on the computer screen.

As Edith chatted, I seemed to be working faster--that is, until she said, "I just wish the Lord would open the door to a publisher for me like He did for you. Imagine how many lives will be touched by your words and be changed by His Word."

Conviction rolled over me. "Oh, Edith," I said, "you

don't know how much your words mean to me. You see, I was only thinking about all the work I had to do to finish the project. I overlooked what God was going to do with it. Thank you for bringing to my attention that He and I are in this together."

As I hung up the phone, I returned to my editing. Edith's call had given me a renewed purpose.

Lord God, knowing that You will be using my work in a special way, I ...

_____

_____

_____

_____

_____

_____

_____

_____

_____

Karen "Lucky" Chole is a free-lance writer and columnist from Mesa, Arizona. Her first book *Facing the Brokenness* — meditations for parents of sexually-abused children — has been accepted by Herald Press.

A VOICE IN THE DARK

Larry Clark

There will be no more gloom for those who were in
distress... The people walking in darkness have seen a great
light.   (Isaiah 9:1-2, KJV)

Once in a while I reflect on my life before I met the
Lord. I kept a diary during one of those dark years. I
was 18, confused, frustrated and bored with life. I filled
page after page with my aimless quest for happiness as
I struggled to please my peers and enjoy their applause.

The following year I found Christ as Saviour and
over the years He has dispelled the darkness of my
mind and flooded me with light. Following some 20
years as a missionary in Mexico, I began to write
non-fiction. Ten more years of writing exhausted my
store of personal experience stories and ideas became
harder to find.

Now the Lord is showing me that short stories are a
wonderful outlet for Christian writers to express their
feelings. In my non-Christian days in high-school, I
didn't know how to fight back. I longed for my peers to
accept me. Instead, I became the butt of dumb jokes
because I was bashful, awkward, and naive.

Now the short story provides me with an offensive

weapon. I can recreate scenes from that painful era and provide Christian answers to the moral and social dilemmas teenagers face today.

The short story leaves me satisfied. It gives me a voice to speak out to troubled youth and also nudges those who still live in darkness.

Dear Jesus, let me see my difficulties and setbacks as ...

_____

_____

_____

_____

_____

_____

_____

_____

_____

_____

Larry Clark lives in Santa Ana, California where he is Assistant Editor at *In Other Words*, the publication of Wycliffe Bible Translators, and a free-lance writer. He has published over 50 articles and one book, *Not Silenced By Darkness*.

THROUGH GOD'S EYES

Teresa J. Cleary

For now we see through a glass, darkly; but then face to face. (1 Corinthians 13:12a, KJV)

"Mom, look!" Micah said, pointing to the back of the cereal box. "See the bear flying a kite?"

I looked at the box only to see a jumble of blue and red lines. "No, I don't see it." I admitted.

"Try these." Micah handed me a pair of red-lensed glasses that had come in the cereal. I put them on and suddenly saw not only the bear, but a girl swinging from a rainbow.

I took off the glasses and put them on again, watching the bear and the girl disappear and reappear. As I did, I realized that Micah's cereal-box treasure was giving me a clear picture of what God intended for my writing.

Just as those red-lensed glasses blocked out the blue lines that hid all the pictures, I want my writing to help others block out the busyness and confusion around them and see God's perfect picture for their lives. I want them to read what I write and experience that "Oh, I see it now!" feeling you get when something finally becomes clear. I want them to see God's love and compassion. I want to help them look at their world and see it through God's eyes.

With that purpose in mind, each time I write, I remember Micah's red-lensed glasses and mentally put on my own pair--the ones with the God-shaped lenses that help me see the hurting world from the Lord's perspective and write to touch that world.

Father God, I see it now. You want me to ...

_____

_____

_____

_____

_____

_____

_____

_____

_____

_____

Teresa Cleary has had over 450 articles published in a wide variety of Christian magazines. She lives in Cincinnati, Ohio with her husband, Tim, and two sons, Micah and Steven.

IT REALLY MEANS ALL THINGS!

Alan Cliburn

And we know that all things work together for good to them that love God, to them who are the called according to his purpose. (Romans 8:28, KJV)

"Oh no!" I thought as I opened my mail. A favorite manuscript had been returned. Again. How many times? I wondered. At least ten rejections of a true story I had thought would be snapped up on the first time out. It was about a woman who had turned her son over to the police for selling drugs to elementary school kids. Only her faith and the support of her Christian friends had kept her sane throughout the ordeal.

"So what do I do with it now?" I asked myself. I re-read the manuscript to see if I had made some major journalistic blunders. No, it seemed to read well.

Never give up! I reminded myself, repeating the message I would tell students at many Christian writers conferences. After all, I had sold one story after fifty rejections and a children's book after ten. Even *Gone With the Wind* made the rounds of publishing houses before it was finally accepted!

So I put the manuscript back into circulation. An

adult Sunday school take-home paper that would have paid $25 sent it right back. It was the last address on my list. My list of Christian adult markets, that is. "Well, why not try a secular publication!" I decided. I had nothing to lose but the postage.

You can guess the ending. Yes, the secular magazine purchased it for $150, but the money was really secondary. When the article, "Incorrigible" came out in print, all the references to Christ and the church had been left in!

But that's only part of it. The last take-home paper that had rejected it had a circulation of several thousand. The cover of the secular magazine, available at newsstands all over the country, announced "Circulation: 5,000,000."

Yes, "All things" also applies to Christian free-lancers!

Father in heaven, grant me wisdom to send ...

Alan Cliburn has been writing professionally since 1961 and has sold thousands of stories to primarily Christian markets, but also to magazines such as *Highlights for Children, Teen*, and *Lady's Circle*. He has taught at many Christian writers conferences, including eight years at Mount Hermon and five years at Biola Writer's Institute. Alan lives in Van Nuys, California.

BUSY HANDS

Jeane E. Clymer

*Whatsoever thy hand findeth to do, do it with thy might:
for there is no work nor device nor knowledge, nor wisdom
in the grave where thou goest.*   (Ecclesiastes 9:10, KJV)

I sat staring at the half-filled page in my typewriter,
my thoughts desert dry. The idea I began with had
blown away in a gust of wind. Then suddenly the sight
of my mother's hands appeared in my mind.

As a youngster I watched her busy hands sew fine
stitches or soothe a child. In her scrubbed kitchen
those hands made fine-grained cakes with
mouth-watering frosting, or kneaded dough for our
bread supply. Sometimes I could help by scattering fat
raisins on sugary cinnamon dough for tempting sweet
rolls.

Holidays meant special delights for others as well as
our own family. She prepared food for the ill, aged,
and the family down the block with financial problems.
The little girl in our neighborhood who had never
owned a new dress received two beautifully-sewn
dresses to start school. Mother kept busy for others.

Her nails were uneven and broken, and her hands
scrubbed red and clean. They would never do for a nail
polish advertisement today, but to the people whose
lives they touched, Mother's hands were beautiful.

Today Mom sits in her wheelchair in a nursing
home. Her once able, busy hands are now blue veined

and restlessly caress each other. They are empty for longer than at any time in her ninety-one years. Helpful hands with nothing to do.

Abruptly, I turned from my memories and saw my own hands idle in my lap, the task the Lord had for them, undone. I began again. Now I had the story for my half-finished page.

My God and Master, help me today to add something of eternal value to ...

_____

_____

_____

_____

_____

_____

_____

_____

Jeane Clymer, a resident of Phoenix, Arizona, is active in Toastmasters, writes fiction and non-fiction, and poetry for friends and contests. Along with three other ladies (The Phoenix Phor), she helped write a 365-page thought-for-the-day calendar which is to be published by Outreach Publications.

PRAY FOR ME

Elaine Wright Colvin

Pray all the time. Ask God for anything in line with the Holy Spirit's wishes. Plead with him, reminding him of your needs, and keep praying earnestly for all Christians everywhere. Pray for me, too, and ask God to give me the right words as I boldly tell others about the Lord.
(Ephesians 6:18-19, TLB)

What a powerful tool we possess as Christian writers and speakers. Our words, in whatever form we use them, have the power to effect a change in other's viewpoints, add to their knowledge, entertain them, or cause them to pause and think about their lifestyles, goals, and eternal destiny. Authors must take special delight in this opportunity to make a mark on the world--even if only one person's life is changed by our message.

Pastor and author Dr. Charles Stanley says, "It is an awesome responsibility to guide others to learn who they are in Christ and to find the resources God has provided for them. That makes it imperative that we, as Christian writers and speakers, pray and stay in touch with God and seek His leading and direction as we preach and write." (The Christian Writer, August 1983)

It was E. M. Bounds who said, "Prayer works so well in a crisis, one wonders why we don't implement it on a regular basis."

Let us pray for each other that we will continue to write and speak boldly for Christ in spite of often distracting circumstances. Pray that we will be wise in our handling of the Word and that God will accomplish His will through each of our writing endeavors.

A Holy Spirit "nudge" to pray for your writing/speaking brother or sister probably comes on the day that the enemy is attacking most viciously with seeds of doubt, discouragement, and defeat. Yes, we really do need each other and especially each other's prayers.

Gracious Lord, let me see things from Your perspective so that I may ...

_____

_____

_____

_____

_____

_____

Elaine Wright Colvin has been active in Christian writing since 1976 as a Christian Writers Consultant, Writers Conference Director, and Director of W.I.N. Writers Information Network, The Professional Association for Christian Writers.
She resides in Bainbridge Island, Washington.

PRAYER WRITING

Shirley Cook

Do not be anxious about anything, but in everything by prayer and petition, with thanksgiving, present your requests to God. (Philippians 4:6, NIV)

Some mornings as I roll that clean white sheet into the typewriter and poise my fingers above the keys, I feel those faceless editors breathing down my neck. Will anyone like my book? What kind of articles do they want? How can I put the thoughts that race through my mind into the right words?

My fingers stiffen, my brain freezes. Suddenly I get a craving for those cookies I baked yesterday. My tension, instead of producing pages of marketable words, has created what is commonly referred to as "writers' block."

In the past I gave in, gobbled a few cookies, and then waited for a better day to begin writing. No more. I've learned that the best way to throw off those fantasy fears and anxieties is to pray--and I do it at the typewriter. I pour out my thoughts, worries and frustrations to God in "prayerwriting." I don't concern myself with punctuation or perfect grammar. I just tell Him everything that concerns me, thank Him for who He is and for the privilege of being a writer. Then I file that "writer's block" away, grind in fresh paper--and what do you know--I wrote this page!

Creator Father, I call on Your promise to supply ...

_____

_____

_____

_____

_____

_____

_____

_____

_____

_____

_____

Shirley Cook is a resident of Stockton, California and the author of nine published books including *Diary of a Fat Housewife* and *Murder on the Fat Express*. She just completed a six-year project, *Bitter Seed*, a historical novel of China and the California Gold Rush.

THE NEVER-ENDING PROJECT

Marsha Crockett

*You show that you are a letter from Christ...written not
with ink but with the Spirit of the living God, not on
tablets of stone, but on tablets of human hearts.*
(2 Corinthians 3:3, NIV)

I always keep an unfinished writing project on the
burner. In fact, I'm working on a project I doubt will
ever be completed in my lifetime. But this one doesn't
require paper and ink--simply a willing heart and a
renewed mind. It's called the composition of my life.

As a writer, I constantly remind myself my best
seller doesn't lie in the words I write, but in the life I
live. Christ living in me takes priority over my own
wisely-contrived words. And when I take my eyes off
that fact, I fail not only as a writer but, more
importantly, as a Christian.

The Corinthian church struggled with this same
problem. They placed great importance on letters of
recommendation required to welcome followers into
their fellowship. They lost sight of Christ's message.

Paul gave them a new focus. He said, "...you are a
letter for Christ...written not with ink but with the Spirit
of the living God, not on tablets of stone but on tablets

of human hearts." (2 Corinthians 3:3, NIV)

Unless my life becomes a letter for Christ, my writing lacks the depth and the power to touch human hearts. I give birth to stillborn words without the Spirit of God living in me. He alone inspires the ideas and the words.

It's a never-ending project -- always needing revisions. But when I allow God to turn my life into His writing instrument and fill me with the ink of His Spirit, then I begin to make a mark for Him on the tablets of human hearts.

Beloved Father, plant Your word deep in my convictions that I might ...

_____

_____

_____

_____

_____

_____

_____

Marsha Crockett is a homemaker with two daughters. She also works part-time with her husband in his PC consulting firm in Chandler, Arizona. She has been published in several Christian publications including *Today's Christian Woman, Aglow,* and *Light & Life*.

REACHING THE CHILDREN

Lou Cross

Come, ye children, hearken unto me; I will teach you the
fear of the Lord. (Psalm 34:11, KJV)

Answering the phone, I recognized the timid voice
of a fourteen-year-old neighbor girl who had left home
and was living on the streets. This night she had no
place to sleep and wanted to know if I would help her.

As a mother and grandmother, I am concerned
about the corruption that permeates our land, captures
the hearts of our children and ruins their lives.
According to statistics, drugs, alcoholism, divorce,
suicide, pornography, and unbelief in God and His
Word are on the increase. Each day our newspapers
announce the many crimes committed the previous day.
All this--happening in a nation that once feared God
and had high moral and ethical standards.

While babysitting my grandchildren one evening, I
suggested we read the Bible.

"Oh, Grandma, the Bible is so boring," was their
frank reply.

"Well then, come and I will tell you a story," I said
leading them up to bed. They listened enthralled while
I told them the beautiful story of creation.

61

These children like to read stories as well as hear them. Since it is impossible for me to spend much time with them in person, I am thankful God has given me the desire to write stories for them and other young people that they might be awakened to the truths found in God's Word. In this way, I can help stem the tide of evil and teach the children to seek God.

Loving God, let me tell a story about ...

_____

_____

_____

_____

_____

_____

_____

_____

_____

_____

Lou Cross, a resident of Phoenix, Arizona, has six children and eleven grandchildren. Her specialty is writing Christian poetry, short stories, and humorous biographical sketches.

WEIGHTED OR FREE?

Shirley Dechaine

Let us throw off everything that hinders and the sin that so easily entangles, and let us run with perseverance the race marked out for us. (Hebrews 12:1, NIV)

Christian writers and speakers often feel we are "weighted down." There are great hindrances to the earnestly-felt conviction that we need to be writing or speaking. What are these hindrances and how can we overcome them?

My personal dilemma involves not only past rejections--an unhappy childhood and a failed marriage, but also the neglect of discipline. I know I have the ability within me to create words that can touch hearts and lives, but the road to effective communication intersects with that of the spiritual disciplines (solitude, meditation, study, prayer) and involves the willingness to become deeply vulnerable.

Some of us experience the weight of a genuine lack of confidence. Because we have not mentally asserted that God has given us a gift, we feel we are under no obligation to write or speak. Yet the encouragement someone has received through something we wrote or spoke attests to this ability--indeed, this calling.

Cultivation of the spiritual disciplines, says Richard Foster in his *Celebration of Discipline*, does not lead us to sackcloth and ashes but to joyful liberation of the inner spirit so that, being set free, nothing can hold us down.

Let us then throw aside anything that hinders us from following God's calling and begin running the race today--with perseverance.

Good Shepherd, grant to me the needed spiritual discipline to ...

_____

_____

_____

_____

_____

_____

_____

_____

_____

Shirley Dechaine is the former owner of a secretarial service and lives in Mesa, Arizona. She is now a school teacher and author of two books: a "Fruit of the Spirit" activity book for children and a devotional book on the Psalms for mothers.

But . . .
Jesus
immediately said to them:
"Take courage! It is I.
            Do not be afraid."

"Lord, if it is you," Peter replied.
"Tell me to come to you on
                the water."

~"Come".

MAT. 14:27-29

LEIGH KNOWLES

BLACK STITCHES

Sandy Dengler

*Then David said to Nathan, "I have sinned against the
Lord." Nathan replied, "The Lord has taken away your
sin. You are not going to die."* (2 Samuel 12:13, KJV)

It was the afghan of the century -- five by seven feet,
seven major panels, great sprays of embroidered
flowers. The project took me nine years to complete.

But wait. The cross-stitch graph for embroidering
the sprays of lovely flowers called for black in the
leaves. Nonsense! This afghan was Spring. Beauty.
Smarter than the instructions, I substituted dark green.
The completed panels looked flat. Oh, they were
pretty, but not beautiful. So I ripped out my dark green
and put in the black as indicated. Instantly the other
colors sprang to life.

Often I find myself begging God to spare me from
all the black stitches. Let the bad things happen to
others. In my search for comfort I forget how necessary
that black is to my own wholeness. And my own
children--I want them to be happy; to be Spring; to be
Beauty. Am I trying too hard to protect them from
those small black stitches that will make them the apple
of God's eye?

A bit of black makes all the difference in the
fictional characters I create, too. A shortcoming here, a
flaw there make them human. Like David, the apple of
God's eye, even heroes need a few dark shadows if they

are to come vividly to life.

Gracious Lord Jesus, let me become vividly alive by being willing to show my ...

_____

_____

_____

_____

_____

_____

_____

_____

_____

_____

Sandy Dengler is working on her thirtieth book, a ghost-writing project. She has made scores of quilts and afghans, most of them with black parts. She makes her home in Ashford, Washington.

THE
SPIRIT
SPEAKS

Pat Egan Dexter

For it is not ye that speak, but the Spirit of your Father who speaketh in you. (Matthew 10:20, KJV)

For many years, before I would begin a writing session, I would meditate on the work I planned to do that day. I did not publish even one small article for the three years, even though I worked everyday, and at times I became most discouraged.

Once I cried out to God to either take away my desire to be a writer or allow me some small measure of success. "What am I to do, Lord?" I asked. And the Lord gave me the above verse. I took that to mean that God would speak through my writing. I decided to continue to be the best writer I could be.

It was another year before I finally sold my first article. Even now after three published books and numerous articles, when too much time goes by without a sale I return to that passage. It reinforces my belief that He means for me to be the best writer I can be at this time, so I should continue to work at it.

Almighty Lord, reinforce daily my belief that I must ...

_____

_____

_____

_____

_____

_____

_____

_____

_____

_____

_____

_____

_____

_____

_____

Pat Egan Dexter is the author of three juvenile books and is a contributing writer to *Guideposts*. She has written extensively for the religious and juvenile markets, including short stories and non-fiction articles, and recently completed a young adult suspense novel. She lives in Mesa, Arizona.

THE GIFT
OF
ENCOURAGEMENT

Dina Donohue

*Each one should use whatever gift he has received to serve
others, faithfully administering God's grace in its various
forms.*   (1 Peter 4:10, NIV)

This past Christmas I noted how many cards and
letters I received from former *Guideposts* authors.
These writers are now my friends and I treasure them.

It's a bit unusual for an editor to establish such
personal ties. How did I accomplish this? It began
years ago at a *Guideposts* editorial meeting when we
decided that each editor should do more than just the
routine work of the magazine.

As a result, John and Elizabeth Sherrill spent a year
in Africa teaching the natives to write inspirational
stories. Other editors pursued special projects. As for
me, I decided to encourage writers to do the best they
could, relying on God.

I truly enjoy the contacts I made with *Guideposts*
authors through my work at writers' conferences and
my evaluation service. Sometimes, though, I'm
frustrated because in helping others achieve success, my
own writing has suffered. A *Guideposts* editor
reassured me, "Maybe this is what God wants you to
do." I like to think it is.

I used to put a few quotations on the bulletin board

above my desk at *Guideposts.* One was from 1 Peter 4:11 to which I added, in humility, a verse that served as a guide for my day and could help all writers: "If anyone speaks, he should do it as one speaking the very words of God. If anyone serves, he should do it with the strength God provides and, for me, if anyone writes, he should do it to further God's kingdom."

Lord, grant me courage to ...

_____

_____

_____

_____

_____

_____

_____

_____

_____

Dina Donohue, former Senior Editor, now a Contributing Editor, has been with *Guideposts* since 1952. The author of many stories and articles, she has spoken and led workshops at numerous writers' conferences throughout the country. She resides in San Diego, California.

THE FRUITFUL TREE

Pauline Dunn

He shall be like a tree planted by the rivers of water, that bringeth forth his fruit in his season; his leaf also shall not wither; and whatsoever he doeth shall prosper.

(Psalms 1:3, KJV)

"Lord, I need help," I prayed, sitting at my typewriter. "I can't settle down to write this morning."

When I smelled the stew simmering in the crockpot, I half rose to dash into the kitchen and stir up an elaborate salad for lunch. No. I settled back again. Better stick with my plan to streamline lunch and gain some writing time.

Outside my window, bees hummed contentedly among the snowy blossoms of the prune-plum tree. Across the yard, a crowd of daffodils raised their heads to gaze at the sun. How I would love to be out-of-doors.

Then my eyes lighted on the pinon tree rising tall and stately in our neighbor's yard, straight trunk pointing toward heaven; cool, dark green needles forming a backdrop for the tender green of the other trees.

Slowly I recited, "He shall be like a tree." Like a

tree! Suddenly it swept over me. Only this morning I had read Psalms one, the Psalm of the blessed man.

"He shall be like a tree planted"— steadfast.

"By the rivers of water"— refreshed by the Holy Spirit.

"That bringeth forth his fruit in his season"— His timing is always right.

"His leaf also shall not wither"— not easily discouraged.

I realized I need, by God's grace and help, to be steadfast like our neighbor's pinon tree—
steadfast in my purpose to write for the Lord. I need to learn to persevere as I pursue the goals I feel He has given me. Refreshed and encouraged by His Spirit, I shall bring forth fruit in season.

Jesus, refresh and encourage my spirit to ...

_____

_____

_____

_____

_____

_____

Pauline Dunn served as a missionary to China, the Philippines, and to the American Indians for 49 years. She and her husband are now retired in the mountains of Prescott, Arizona where she enjoys public speaking and writing her experiences.

HIDING THE WORD IN YOUR HEART

June Eaton

I have hidden your word in my heart.
(Psalm 119:11, NIV)

Katherine Paterson, award-winning author of young adult novels, was asked what literary work had most influenced her as a writer. Without equivocation she answered, "The stories that have shaped me most are the stories of the Bible."[1]

Though Paterson never quotes Bible verses nor overtly includes the salvation message in her stories, one can hear the beauty and truths of Scripture echoing throughout the pages of her books. Considered a secular novelist, she was once a missionary to Japan, and she has spent a lifetime hiding the Word in her heart.

It may seem obvious to suggest that Christian writers and speakers follow the example of David in Psalm 119 as Paterson has, storing up the treasures of the Bible in their hearts. Most Christians profess an acquaintance with biblical content. Yet for many, the study of Scripture remains an intellectual exercise. God's words reside in the head instead of the heart.

What is needed instead is a love-motivated reading,

studying, meditating, and digesting of Scripture so that the Word becomes part of our innermost beings. The more Scripture we have hidden in our hearts, the more of it we can share on an unconscious level through our writing and speaking.

Our purpose is not to astound others with our knowledge of the Bible, nor to pepper our manuscripts and speeches with Scriptural quotes, but to gain a foundation — a rock upon which to build our lives and our work.

We can do that through a deep and personal interaction with His Word. Only then will *our* words become informed and illuminated by Scripture, reaching out to others with the aroma of Christ...with a word to sustain the weary.

[1]*Worlds of Childhood*, William Zinsser, ed., Houghton-Mifflin, 1990, p. 159.

My Lord and Savior, help me to pursue You in ...

_____

_____

_____

_____

_____

June Eaton has been the Director of Christian Writers Institute and its annual writers conference for seven years. She writes curriculum, book reviews, fiction, and articles for adults and children from her home in Villa Park, Illinois.

GOD'S BECKONING THROUGH NATURE

Frances Engle

And God saw everything that he had made and behold it was very good. (Genesis 1:31, RSV)

When I said "yes" to camping, I had no idea it would take our family to every mainland state of the United States. Or that writing about those trips would unveil one of my gifts.

In Glacier National Park, we sat among shiny, deep gold buttercups for a picnic beside an energetic stream. The lofty snow-capped giants of the Rockies dwarfed the existence of my personal world, but I felt God leading me.

I stooped low to look at mounds of tiny pink, blue, yellow, and white tundra flowers growing in little soil. They had survived the harsh winds of winter. Their colors of courage reminded me that we, too, can grow from faith as small as a mustard seed.

From the top of a mountain peak, I stood overlooking lakes and reservoirs far below. They shrank to mere pockets of water, and rivers to slight penciled lines. Molded glaciers lay in the cirques of mountain slopes. Verdant grasses and trees, acres of multi-colored wild flowers converged to form a painting of incredible loveliness. The design of God's garden has no equal. And this was no small rose garden.

I saw why He proclaimed the work of His creation good. It is — and breathtaking! I was drawn close to the heartbeat of God within the folds of nature. Overwhelming adoration flowed through me, and I cried, "How great Thou art!"

I'm excited to write about the beauty of God's creation!

God, nature has revealed ...

_____

_____

_____

_____

_____

_____

_____

Frances Engle writes a monthly article for Senior Life Magazine, and is the author of a book, *Three Bonus Years*, about her neighbor who had cancer with thirty to sixty days to live. She resides in Richmond, Indiana.

MY TIME OR YOURS, LORD?

Betty Steele Everett

My times are in your hands.
(Psalms 31:15, NIV)

Since David followed these words with a plea for protection from his enemies, I had always assumed "My times" meant only the length of our lives.

Then my husband took early retirement. Suddenly the time I had to write--alone and unhampered--was completely gone. My husband wanted us to do things together.

"Lord," I prayed, "I can't stop writing! I love it, and remember, I'm writing for You! Shouldn't I just say 'no' when he wants me to go places and do things with him instead of writing?"

The answer seemed immediate. "I have others to write for me; you're the only one who can be a companion to your husband."

It was not the answer I wanted! I struggled to keep to my old writing schedule, only to see it gradually fall apart. I was torn and confused. While I thoroughly enjoyed the hours with my husband, I missed my writing time terribly.

I kept praying. Months passed. My production

dropped lower, but my husband and I were closer than ever. I decided to stop fighting; I turned my times over to the Lord.

To my surprise, my production slowly started to rise. My husband began to find things to do downtown for an hour each morning. It wasn't the time I'd had before, but it was free writing time! The Lord had given me time both to write and to enjoy my husband's retirement.

No writer ever has enough time to write, but our times, like David's are in His hands.

Lord Jesus, let me know when to ...

_____

_____

_____

_____

_____

_____

_____

_____

Betty Steele Everett has had more than 4000 short stories and articles and five books published. She has taught at six Christian writers' conferences and spoken before many church and writers' groups. She lives in Defiance, Ohio.

GOD'S MESSENGER

Diane Boice Fillmore

[God's voice may be heard] if there is for the hearer a messenger...,an interpreter, one among a thousand to show to man what is right for him [how to be upright and in right standing with God]. (Job 33:23, AMP)

The book of Job had always been a depressing one for me. Its constant emphasis on suffering, pain and loneliness left me hungry for cheerier reading material. Until, I read Job 33:23. That one verse renewed, refreshed and reconfirmed my calling as a communicator of God's truth.

Job and his legendary suffering share much in common with the people we encounter every day. Our audiences, our readers, our co-workers, our neighbors, and our families are all intimately acquainted with pain. Along with Job they say, "Life is hard, full of hurt. What have I done to deserve the unhappiness, loneliness, or illness that touches my life? Why do these things happen?"

Most people seldom vocalize their questions about suffering as eloquently as Job did, but the thoughts still dwell in their hearts. To wonder about pain is part of the human condition.

That is why we are called as Christian communicators. We have been assigned to be the messengers, the interpreters, the one among a thousand who can help make sense out of the human condition.

We are those who speak on God's behalf. When we saturate our communication in Biblical truth and wisdom, then we are able to help hurting people receive God's healing and comfort. That is our task.

It is the awareness of the importance of our job that keeps me pounding the keyboard and mounting the podium. How about you? Did you know that you are God's messenger?

Father, grant me wisdom to recognize the message I'm to
...

_____

_____

_____

_____

_____

_____

_____

_____

Diane Boice Fillmore combines her duties as Associate Editor of *The Christian Communicator* with free-lance writing and desktop publishing. She and her husband and two sons live in La Puente, California.

We rejoice in the hope of the Glory of God.

Not only so, but we rejoice in our sufferings, because we know that suffering produces perserverance; perserverance, character; and character, hope.

And hope does not disappoint us, because God has poured out His love into our hearts by the Holy Spirit whom He has given us.

ROMANS 5:2-5

LEIGH KNOWLES

THE HEART'S ABUNDANCE

Reg A. Forder

Out of the abundance of the heart the mouth speaketh.
(Matthew 12:34, KJV)

This scripture may also be paraphrased, "Out of the abundance of the heart the pen writeth." We will probably never be a successful writer or speaker if we try communicating about things we've never experienced, don't really feel, or in which we have no genuine interest.

One day a salesman came into my office and attempted to sell me on a long distance telephone service. The benefits he listed were so attractive I was ready to go for it. It was then I learned that he was not, nor ever had been, on that service himself. He didn't make the sale.

To share the good news with others, we must first be sure we ourselves have a solid relationship with Christ. We're going to have difficulty convincing people of the reality of Christ if we haven't found Him to be real in our own lives. Any doubts we have will creep through in our writings.

It's difficult for us to keep our true thoughts and feelings hidden. No matter how hard we work at concealment, what's inside comes out in what we say, how we act, how we react, and what we write.

If we don't like what is coming from us and displaying itself on paper, it may indicate a spiritual check-up is needed.

However, if Jesus is first in our lives and dwelling in our hearts at all times, it is out of that abundance that we will write and God will bless our ministry. For the Christian writer, the pen is the pulpit.

Heavenly Father, give me spiritual eyes to ...

_____

_____

_____

_____

_____

_____

_____

_____

_____

_____

Reg Forder is the Director of the annual Arizona Christian Writers Conference in Phoenix, Arizona. He has written one book and over 100 articles. He is the former editor of Singles World and Good News publications.

A GIFT

Joy P. Gage

They helped everyone his neighbor; and...the carpenter
encouraged the goldsmith.   (Isaiah 41:6-7a, KJV)

Three months after the release of our co-authored book, my husband and I received a Christmas package from my sister and brother-in-law. Christmas was still a week away, but since the tag read "To our favorite authors," curiosity got the best of us.

Inside we found a beautifully-worked needlepoint of Psalm 102:18: "This will be written for the generation to come, that a people yet to be created may praise the Lord." We knew at once this was a gift of encouragement as well as a gift of love.

Encouragement is a lifeblood of the writer. There are times we feel a desperate need for a transfusion, not so much praise and pats on the back, but affirmation that we are on the right track. We need someone to validate our decision to spend hours behind the typewriter cut off from people.

Nothing brings encouragement like letters from readers telling you that what you have written has helped them to make a life-changing decision, or given them cause to praise the Lord.

Sometimes we have to encourage ourselves. Look at the circulation of the last magazine to publish one of your articles. Somewhere among those readers you have had a ministry. Remember also that this year's royalty check affirms the fact that through writing you are reaching more people than you could possibly reach any other way.

If these facts fail to encourage you, or if you haven't yet made that first sale, there is one more thing you can do. Copy Psalm 102:18 — no need to needlepoint it — and tack it above your typewriter.

My Father, grant me boldness to encourage ...

_____

_____

_____

_____

_____

_____

_____

_____

_____

_____

Joy P. Gage of San Rafael, California is a speaker, writer, and novelist who has authored and co-authored (with her husband) 12 books. A pastor's wife, she also finds time to speak at conferences and lead women's retreats, parents' groups, and special interest seminars throughout the United States.

BECAUSE HE HELPS

Dorothy Galde

Because the Lord God helps me, I will not be dismayed; therefore I have set my face like a flint to do His will, and I know that I will triumph. (Isaiah 50:7, TLB)

Doesn't this verse fill the soul with energy and assurance? We know it is God's will that, as writers, we should speak out for Him. It is the Great Commission. And surely, "From the abundance of the heart, the mouth speaketh." (Matthew 12:34)

John tells us, "we speak what we know." (3:1) That is simple, but profound. In ten years of teaching college English, I found the need to reassure many students who felt they had nothing worthwhile to say.

Each Christian writer has a unique message. No one else has had identical experiences or the same responses to those experiences.

The Lord has placed each of us in a special spot in His vineyard. He has given us capabilities, talents, and preferences. Although the separate entities that make us up are common to all people, the combination of all that we are is unlike any other.

As we reflect on life through the magnifying glass of God's Word, our thoughts about God and our reactions to His movement in our lives may answer a deep need in the hearts of many readers.

If we don't say it, it won't be said — not in the way we alone can say it.

Instead of being dismayed at the thought of writing an article or book that God has pressed into our hearts, let us set our faces like flint, and *do* the project with God's help.

Dear Lord, with Your guidance ...

_____

_____

_____

_____

_____

_____

_____

_____

_____

Dorothy Galde, a resident of Prescott, Arizona, has had ten books published, including high school English workbooks. She was on the founding faculty of Yavapai College, where she taught English for ten years. Dorothy also speaks occasionally and has taught at Christian writer's seminars.

CALL ANSWERED

Lucille Gardner

Call unto me, and I will answer thee.
(Jeremiah 33:3, KJV)

I rolled the paper into my typewriter. Recalling the verse above, I breathed a prayer that God would help me edit my words. Then I reread my four handwritten paragraphs, feeling a sense of responsibility to unknown persons who would use the devotional guide. Would my words minister to their needs and bring vibrant meaning to the assigned scripture?

I started typing. After completing several sentences, I stopped abruptly. I felt I must take time right then for my own daily Bible reading.

Turning the pages of my *Secret Place* quarterly to that day's date, I caught my breath as I looked at the title "Unseen Friend." The devotional I had written dealt with life's true values, the unseen intangibles, but I had left out the most important one — Christ, the Unseen Friend.

The scripture passage I read was familiar to me, but that day I had a new appreciation for its message and a sense of wonder. God had answered my plea for help by pointing out the all-important words I had omitted.

I returned to my desk with renewed determination to always ask for God's guidance before embarking on any writing project. I finished my typing with deep gratitude and a realization of God's presence. I had called upon Him and He had answered.

Holy Father, I call out to You to ...

_____

_____

_____

_____

_____

_____

_____

_____

_____

_____

Lucille Gardner wrote numerous poems for Christian and secular publication, and also authored the book, *There is Hope*, which sold more than 135,000 copies. On December 11, 1989, Lucille went home to her Lord. Her family has established a scholarship fund in her memory for poets attending the Mt. Hermon Christian Writer's Conference.

IMMORTAL WORDS

William H. Gentz

The grass withers and the flowers fail, but the word of our God stands forever. (Isaiah 40:8, NIV)

This verse from Isaiah is talking about the Word of God. But I'm convinced that there is a sense in which our words too are immortal. In the April 1985 issue of *The Writer*, Roger Caras wrote in the "Off the Cuff" column:

Our typewriters will rust, the buildings we work in as we write will crumble, even if they are made of marble, or they will be bulldozed away. The only things that will survive, if only in scraps and shards, are our thoughts, our words. Our biological line could end one day. It could be as if we were never here, except for our words...I think this crack at immortality is one of the real perks of being a writer.

This thought is going through my head now in reference to our work as Christian writers. If we are dedicated to God, surely as we let him lead us, his Word is flowing through us onto paper and, if so, our words are immortal in their own way.

Therefore, we must test what we write against what God has written in his Word. Also we need to apply ourselves to our craft with a spirit of dedication to doing God's will in our time.

O Lord, with a spirit of dedication, I commit ...

_____

_____

_____

_____

_____

_____

_____

_____

_____

_____

_____

William H. Gentz, a Lutheran pastor, lives in New York City and has spend most of his career in publishing as an editor of books and magazines. He is the author or editor of six books, including *Writing to Inspire* and the *Religious Writers Marketplace*, and a number of magazine articles. He has taught writer's workshops in several states as well as a class in writing at the New York School of the Bible.

THE TAX OF TENURE

Jeannette Clift George

And I heard the voice of the Lord saying, "Whom shall I send, and who will go for us? Then I said, "Here am I! Send me." (Isaiah 6:8, RSV)

I am in a ministry which includes Christian theater, writing, and public speaking. I can't think of any better way to live the life of God's opportunity.

However, there are times when the work becomes tedious, the results humiliating, the tensions frustrating. For such a time, God has a great principle.

God prepares His ministers well. For instance, Isaiah. God convicted him, called him, cleansed him and commanded him. Then God gave to his newly appointed missionary a preview of what his work would be like. He said, "You will speak to people who won't hear and obey, who won't see and follow, who won't taste and cry for more!" Isaiah's responding question is frequently the contemporary minister's question: "How long?"

Our glowing picture of what a ministry would be can lose its glow in the midst of its reality. Up to our halos in hopelessness, we ask Isaiah's question, "How long am I to do this?" God's answer is as pertinent as the

95

question —"As long as there are people to hear!"

In the occasional dips and deeps of my work, I find comfort in God's brisk answer. God brushes away sentiment and gives substance. Sentiment may lose its shadings but substance assures celebration. God reminds us that His gift of tenure includes our tax of endurance. There are those who hear, that is the market of our call. In obedience to Him, there will be joy in the doing.

How long? As long as there are people to hear.

Lord God, I hear You saying to me ...

_____

_____

_____

_____

_____

_____

_____

_____

Jeannette Clift George is the founder and Artistic Director of the A.D. Players, a Houston-based Christian theater company which offers plays throughout the world. Mrs. George's extensive background in professional theater includes acting off-Broadway and touring with the New York Shakespeare Company. Her film debut was portraying Corrie ten Boom in World Wide Pictures' "The Hiding Place."

FINDING GOD'S WILL

Lynne Gessner

*Lead me in thy truth, and teach me; for thou art the God
of my salvation; on thee do I wait all the day.*
(Psalms 25:5, KJV)

Early in my career, my writing was a continual
struggle. Ideas did not come easily. Maybe, I thought,
it was not God's plan for me to be a writer. I prayed
and read my Bible daily, imploring God to show me His
will for my life. But even after heart-felt prayer, my
writing seemed bland.

One night as I prayed, I realized that I was asking
God to lead me, but I was still doing what I wanted to
do -- write. So I cleaned my home office and closed the
door. The above verse was my constant prayer.

Weeks went by. Occasionally I glanced at my office
door, yearning to get back to writing. I continued to
pray. Then one day I got an idea for a story and the
urge to write was too strong to resist. I wrote for hours.
What I wrote sparkled with life and suddenly I knew
God was leading me back to my writing. This had been
His will all along, but He wanted me to realize my
inspiration came from Him, not from myself. Since
then I've looked to God for ideas, and my writing has

progressed far beyond my original dreams.

Dear Jesus, You are my inspiration to ...

_____

_____

_____

_____

_____

_____

_____

_____

_____

_____

_____

Lynne Gessner is the author of eleven published novels and over 200 short stories, articles and essays. She also teaches writing at Rio Salado Community College in Scottsdale, Arizona, leads an annual seminar on picture book writing, and speaks at seminars and schools all over Arizona.

SHARE MY SECURITY BLANKET

Jeanette Gilge

Do not be anxious about anything, but in everything, by prayer and petition, with thanksgiving, present your requests to God. (Philippians 4:6, NIV)

And we know that in all things God works for the good of those who love him, who have been called according to his purpose. (Romans 8:28, NIV)

You have probably seen a number of blanket-dragging tots. I certainly have. When Mommy leaves, thunder rattles the windows, or a finger is pinched, they clutch that precious blanket.

I also have a security blanket; in fact, I have two. They're not made from fluffy Orlon or soft cotton, but they're every bit as comforting.

When an editor phones and says, "The committee will make a decision on your manuscript next week;" when a deadline looms near but ideas won't come; when my royalty check is so late I fear it may be lost; or when rejections come but checks don't, I cling to the above scriptures.

I've seen blankets so worn, one could count the snuggles left in them. Not mine! Mine will never wear out because God's Word never loses its power.

But best of all, I can share them with you and still not lose one bit of their comfort.

Father God, I trust in the knowledge that all things work together for ...

_____

_____

_____

_____

_____

_____

_____

_____

_____

_____

Jeanette Gilge is the author of the *Never Miss a Sunset* Pioneer Family Series, published by David C. Cook. She's also a writing instructor and speaker and makes her home in Ogema, Wisconsin.

ANOINTED

TO

WRITE

Peter E. Gillquist

Now therefore, go, and I will be with your mouth and teach you what you shall say. (Exodus 4:12, NKJV)

In this, God's great promise to Moses, we in the New Covenant have the same assurance given to each one of us. The Lord goes on record as saying He will teach us how to speak His Word. We know this as "the anointing of the Spirit" to effectively communicate the Gospel.

Those of us who are preachers have experienced time and time again that the Holy Spirit — often in those times that seem the darkest — will touch our hearts, minds, and lips, and give us the words to say. By God's grace, I have known countless times when I seem to be "bourne along" by the Holy Spirit in my sermons. Anointed preaching, if I may paraphrase, is when it is no longer I who speaks, but Christ who speaks in me.

The good news is that this same anointing is available for Christian writers. As with preaching, sometimes it takes us ten or fifteen minutes of writing before we sense it begins to flow. But if we're relying upon the Holy Spirit and walking in His truth, flow it will!

When you sit down to write, ask the Lord for His power and insight as you begin to express on paper the things that He is speaking by His Holy Spirit to your heart. There is an anointing to write. Believe Him for it.

My God and Master, anoint me to ...

_____

_____

_____

_____

_____

_____

_____

_____

_____

Peter E. Gillquist, of Isla Vista, California, is the author of numerous books including *Love is Now, Becoming Orthodox*, and *Metropolitan Philip: His Life and His Dreams.* He was senior book editor at Thomas Nelson from 1975-86, and as an Orthodox priest serves as Director of Missions and Evangelism for the Antiochian Orthodox Church and as Publisher of *AGAIN Magazine.*

WORDS IN DUE SEASON

Louis R. Goodgame

A man hath joy by the answer of his mouth, and a word spoken in due season, how good is it!

(Proverbs 15:23, KJV)

I couldn't understand it, which is not uncommon for a nineteen-year-old, fresh out of the Army. God had saved me while in the service and then sent me to a Christian college. Since He was guiding my life, why was it harder to be a Christian in college than in the service?

This was my first experience in a Bible school and I loved it. But as I began to compare myself with those godly students, doubts arose. I questioned, Why am I still sinning? It certainly was more comfortable to measure myself against my G.I. buddies.

Attempting to see some growth, I started keeping track of my sins. I listed sins I had overcome, sins currently being resisted, and finally, those sins I honestly wasn't struggling with. After several weeks of "sin-cording" it dawned on me that I was losing the sin battle. Sins were sprouting up faster than I could weed them out. I wouldn't live long enough to conquer my mountain of sins! Being lost was bad, but if in the process I also lost out on the pleasures of sin, that was terrible.

I packed my bag and took a bus to a college that had offered me a football scholarship. Somehow, my New Testament was in my pocket and I started reading it. The promise of Luke 12:32, "Fear not, little flock; for it is your Father's good pleasure to give you the kingdom," erased my fears. With this assurance, I returned to the Christian college.

I was so thankful Luke wrote the words that helped keep me on the right path. Christian writers, too, have the privilege — and responsibility — of writing "words in due season" that can make a difference in the lives of people.

Gracious Lord, I seek Your promise to ...

_____

_____

_____

_____

_____

_____

_____

Louis R. Goodgame is the author of the book, *Delightful Discipline*, a teacher (4 years church school, 26 years public), and a volunteer chaplain's assistant at Pelican Bay State Prison. He lives in Crescent City, California.

LIVING WORDS

Donna Goodrich

[S]he being dead, yet speaketh.
(Hebrews 11:4, KJV)

I sat beside the deathbed of my mother. Not only was I losing my Mom, but also my best friend. I thought of the verse, "Precious in the sight of the Lord is the death of his saints" (Psalm 116:15) and tried to visualize the Lord soon greeting this precious saint. The Lord had prepared her for this during the past year. She was ready to go, but I wasn't ready to let her.

My mother had been the one to encourage me in my early years of writing when the rejections slips came. And it was she who rejoiced with me over sales of articles and books.

I finally left my mother's side for the last time. After her death, when I returned to my hometown to go through her things, my brother handed me an enormous box marked, "Save for Donna."

I opened the box and inside were clippings collected over many years — quotations, anecdotes, and poetry. Written on each was the date and name of the magazine or newspaper the clippings were taken from. It was better than inheriting a gold mine.

How like Mom! As she had shared her ideas and prayers before, she would continue helping me, though gone. "Even so," I prayed, "may my words and writings live on to help others, long after I am gone."

Beloved Father, may Your Word be my words and ...

_____

_____

_____

_____

_____

_____

_____

_____

_____

_____

Donna Goodrich has published ten books and over 400 articles, short stories, poems, and devotionals. She is the founder of the Phoenix and Mesa (Arizona) Christian Writers Clubs, and the author of a 48-page booklet on "How to Start and Lead a Christian Writers Club." In 1982 she began the annual Arizona Christian Writers Seminar. A resident of Mesa, Arizona, she owns a tax and secretarial service, leads small writing workshops in Arizona and other states, and also teaches at writers conferences.

A WRITER'S GARDEN

Alice Graham

And the Lord shall guide thee continually...and thou shalt be like a watered garden, like a spring of water whose waters fail not.   (Isaiah 58:11, KJV)

As God needed Adam to care for the Garden of Eden, so He gives us custody of the seed-thoughts He sows in the garden of our minds. It is our mission to dress and keep it.

A seed-thought drifted into my mind but it did not grow. It fell on the stony ground of hard prejudices. With the Lord's guidance the "waters that fail not" softened the mental soil and a sprout worked its way into the light of understanding. Inspired to research the subject, I changed that soil into good ground. The seed flourished like the mustard seed and bird songs emanated from its branches.

The branches reached out in all directions. The writing had no form. It needed my blue pencil to cut away the rambling offshoots and give it shape and symmetry. My blue pencil became a pruning hook, not a spear.

When I finished, I looked at the story I had created and saw it had the attributes of the Garden of Eden:

harmony, beauty and a sense of peace. It would give nourishing food for thought to its readers.

Creator Father, grant me harmony, beauty, and a sense of peace to ...

_____

_____

_____

_____

_____

_____

_____

_____

_____

_____

_____

Alice Graham lives in Phoenix, Arizona. She writes inspirational articles and poetry, teaches classes in creative writing, and conducts workshops.

CONVERSATIONS WITH THE LORD

Elaine Hardt

Lord, teach us to pray.
(Luke 11:1, KJV)

The house was quiet and cool. I sat at the kitchen table sipping my morning cup of tea and having my personal quiet time. I began with prayer--but stopped short a minute later, realizing my prayer sounded like the grocery list posted on the refrigerator door. I was bringing to the Lord a regular list of wants and do's and don'ts.

Suddenly in my mind's eye I saw the Lord. Of all things, He was sitting in our big overstuffed chair in the living room. Then He lovingly called my name.

Immediately I knew how shallow my prayer life had become. I had been missing out on the wonderful blessing of enjoying the Lord's presence. Now my prayer became a conversation. And praise welled up within me as I felt completely surrounded by His incredible love.

I realized that, although I have a "personal relationship with Christ," I had slipped into formalism in my prayer life.

When I take time to remember Who I am talking with when I pray, my whole day goes better. My outlook on the problems and perplexities of the world takes on a new perspective. My writing has a new purpose.

Loving God, my new purpose is ...

_____

_____

_____

_____

_____

_____

_____

_____

_____

_____

_____

Elaine Hardt is the author of six published books, nearly 60 articles, and numerous poems. She currently teaches third grade at a Phoenix, Arizona public school, as well as an evening class at Arizona College of the Bible. She also speaks to churches, parenting groups, and children's classes.

BE STILL, MY SOUL

A. F. Harper

*You are mine. When you pass through the deep waters, I
will be with you; your troubles will not overwhelm you.*
(Isaiah 43:1-2, TEV)

During a routine medical check, my doctor
confronted me with the possibility of leukemia. "I want
you to see the hematologist for future blood analysis,"
he told me. When I went from the office back to the
lab with the order for further tests, there it was in print,
with the doctor's checkmark in front of it — leukemia.

For eight days the specter of blood cancer hung
over our heads, but our Christian faith buoyed us up.

While waiting in the hospital for a sonogram, I
finished a small book I had been reading. Through this
Christian writer, God gave me courage. At the bottom
of page 13 were the words, "If we do not lose our faith,
we do not lose our strength."

God's writer helped us again during our period of
waiting. The scheduled devotional included, "Do not be
afraid — I will save you...When you pass through the
deep waters, I will be with you; your troubles will not
overwhelm you...For I am the Lord your God." (Isaiah
43:1-2, TEV)

At our family worship on the morning we were to
get the diagnosis from the doctor, my wife said, "Let me
show you the words God gave to me." From one of
God's poet she read:

Be still, my soul; the Lord is on thy side.
Bear patiently the cross of grief or pain;
Leave to thy God to order and provide.
In ev'ry change He faithful will remain.

At 10:30 that morning the doctor said, "I have good news. We did not find the bone marrow as bad as we expected. We will want to keep a check on the blood count, but the problem is not serious enough at this point to require any treatment."

I praise God! I praise Him for His promises given in writing to us in Scripture. I am glad for our Christian faith. I rejoice for Christian writers who put their faith into prose and song. I praise God.

O healing Christ, I have good news to tell which is ...

A.F. Harper, author of *Holiness and High Country* and general editor of *The Wesley Bible* has served as executive editor of the Department of Church Schools for the Church of the Nazarene and holds the title of Professor of Christian Education, Emeritus at Nazarene Theological Seminary.

NEVER ALONE

Sally Hawthorne

Sojourn in this land and I will be with you and bless you.
(Genesis 26:3, NAS)

It wasn't exactly the Holiday Inn. However, after traveling all day on narrow trails in the High Andes, our family was not too choosy about our overnight accommodations — sleeping bags spread on the rocky bank of a river.

Normally we never would have opted to spend a night miles from anywhere, in the company of the rough muleteers who were leading us and our pack animals to our mission station.

How could we just turn over and close our eyes, knowing that while we slept they were capable of stealing away with all our earthly goods?

Then across my troubled mind tiptoed the above Bible verse we had claimed when we departed for South America.

As I began to relax, I knew that in the years ahead I'd tell others that they never have to feel alone, either. They can experience God's comforting presence. I have done this by means of fiction — and my characters do the talking.

You may be a child-rearer, computer expert, teacher...this is where you sojourn. As you speak out of your heart, presenting your particular God-given message — whether in well-researched articles or in the garb of fiction -- you can rely upon Him to add His weight to your words.

Someone out there is in need of encouragement, direction, ideas, a second wind. Trust the Lord to make you a voice He can use for His glory.

Good Shepherd, help me share my God-given message which is ...

_____

_____

_____

_____

_____

_____

_____

_____

_____

Sally Hawthorne is the author of two published books, over one hundred stories, and a family history co-authored with her husband. She also enjoys giving illustrated talks. She lives in Phoenix, Arizona.

THE WRITER'S PRAYER

Dennis Hensley

The meek also shall increase their joy in the Lord, and the poor among men shall rejoice in the Holy One of Israel.
(Isaiah 29:10, KJV)

Lord, remind me daily of how truly insignificant even my greatest works are. Help me to maintain a perspective of things which makes me realize that alone I am nothing, but through You even as nothing I can be something.

As I strive to find my something, make me mindful that I lack an elephant's strength and a flea's agility. Remind me that a peacock is more beautiful, a butterfly more delicate, a rabbit more sensitive.

Alarm me with the currency of the Scripture which warns that my years shall be three score and ten...at best. Shame me with the reminders of how much time I have already squandered. Forgive me for the cowardice in not living a bolder life for You.

Burn into my memory, O timeless God, the records of Samson's weakness, Solomon's folly, Jonah's fear and David's infidelity lest I even for a moment attempt to set myself up as an example for others to admire and emulate.

Let me begin my day fearing to step out of bed unless You are there to support me. Let me stand at noon with a bowed head expressing gratitude for a day of success unmerited by my works but allotted nevertheless by Your grace. Let me close the day on my knees confessing my inadequacies and admitting my frailties.

Gracious Lord Jesus, help me to maintain a perspective of ...

_____

_____

_____

_____

_____

_____

_____

_____

_____

Dr. Dennis E. Hensley is the author of 26 books, including *Money Wise* and *The Freelance Writer's Handbook*. His 2,500 articles have appeared in *Reader's Digest*, *The Writer*, and *The War Cry*, as well as numerous newspapers. In 1991 he served as "Writer in Residence" and Director of the Creative Writing Program at Furman University in Greenville, South Carolina. He lives in Fort Wayne, Indiana.

This is what the
Lord says ~
"Heaven is my throne
and the Earth is my footstool.
Where is the house
you will build for Me?
Where will My
resting place be?
Has my hand not made
all these things,
and so they came into being?" declares
the Lord.
"This is the one I esteem:
he who is humble,
contrite in spirit
and trembles
at my Word."

ISAIAH 66: 1-2

A NEW SONG

Ethel Herr

Sing to Him a new song; play skillfully with a shout of joy.
(Psalm 33:3, NAS)

We expect two things of a great musician — a bright, unique rendition and a skilled performance. These elements enhance the message and bring honor to the composer of the music. In the same way God and our readers have the right to expect from us as writers a new song played skillfully.

A new song is something fresh and exciting shared on paper. Nothing is drier or more deadly than a stale testimony or a cliched rehash of some time-worn concept. A new song never comes easily or glibly. It is born only in a heart that stays constantly in touch with God by digging deeper truths from the Word, growing in practical holiness, hungering and thirsting after God Himself.

A new song played skillfully displays disciplined craftsmanship. A musician pours hundreds of hours into tedious practice in preparation for each stage performance. No one considers those hours wasted. Neither should we feel our hours are wasted when we struggle with unpublishable manuscripts in the process

119

of preparing to write a few literary gems. The gems thus produced, like a brilliant musical performance, enhance our message and bring honor to the Author of the truth we share.

But there is more. We are to play skillfully with a shout of joy. God plans each manuscript to be not only fresh and well-crafted. It is to be an exuberant overflow of a heart profoundly in love with Him.

Almighty God, let me express my new song by ...

_____

_____

_____

_____

_____

_____

_____

_____

Ethel Herr of Sunnyvale, California, is a free-lance writer, writing teacher and retreat speaker. She is author of six books, including *Chosen Women of the Bible* and *An Introduction to Christian Writing*, and founder and director of the Literature Ministry Prayer Fellowship, a network of writers, editors and booksellers enabling them to pray for each other's ministry needs.

DEPENDENCE

Leona Hertel

I can do all things through Christ who strengthens me.
(Philippians 4:13, KJV)

"I'm a writer!"
The first time I said this, I could not believe my ears. How did I dare make such a claim? True, I did write an article every month as editor for the Radio Bible Class Newsletter, but did that make me a writer?

Then readers began to write comments about these articles and I realized the Lord had used my words to minister to them. That's the ecstasy of writing.

There's another side to the coin, the agony — those times when the well is dry and the mind goes blank. The paper in the typewriter doesn't move even one space.

I'm acutely aware of my own inadequacy. In myself I'm helpless and sometimes hopeless. Then the words of the above verse remind me of my dependence on the One who is my help. We're in partnership, and when I am weak He gives the strength. When I lack wisdom, He enlightens my mind with a message from His Word.

Several years ago I met a husband and wife who told me they prayed for me every day that the Lord will direct my thoughts and give me fresh ideas for my writing. I am blessed to have such faithful, silent partners who minister by prayer on my behalf.

So in the strength of the Lord and the prayers of my friends, I rejoice in the privilege of sharing through the use of words, something that will bless, comfort, or encourage a needy heart.

Boldly but humbly I now can say, "I'm a writer."

Lord, give me strength to ...

_____

_____

_____

_____

_____

_____

_____

_____

_____

_____

Leona Hertel of Grand Rapids, Michigan served as the personal secretary to Dr. M. R. DeHaan, founder and teacher of the Radio Bible Class. She was the editor of and contributor to the Bible Class Newsletter, and the editor and compiler of several books. Leona has had many articles published in Christian magazines including *Moody Monthly* and *The Christian Reader.* Currently she is Coordinator of the Maranatha Christian Writers' Seminar.

SAY "YES!" TO PRIORITIES

Mona Gansberg Hodgson

Not everyone who says to Me, 'Lord, Lord,' will enter the kingdom of heaven, but only he who does the will of my Father who is in heaven. (Matthew 7:21, NIV)

MORNING HAS BROKEN — far too early and I've been staying up far too late. My alarm clock finds me wishing to be rescued from this hectic schedule.

I've done it again. I said "yes" too often. For some of us, volunteering can become a career in itself. I can hear the ringing phone now.

"Hello. Volunteer speaking. You especially need me? Oh, you're right. Somebody has to do it. Uh-um-well, sure. Why not?"

Why should a simple "no" turn into a speech impediment? I can pronounce it clearly around pushy salespeople, and I can tell my teenagers to say "no" to their peers. But somehow saying "no" to "worthy causes" sets a chain reaction into motion. My lips freeze, my speech becomes slurred, and "no" bounces off the roof of my mouth and back down into my voice box.

Don't get me wrong, there are times when we should say, "Yes." Likewise, the answer "No" has its proper place. A place that is too often obscure.

Are you called to write? Do you have difficulty finding the time or energy? Our lifestyles of frenzy mandate that we make time, for it won't be found. Perhaps a fresh and prayerful look at our priorities is a daily prescription to be filled by the Great Physician.

Jesus, please guide me in selecting Your priorities in the following activities ...

_____

_____

_____

_____

_____

_____

_____

_____

_____

Mona Hodgson of Cottonwood, Arizona is the poetry instructor for Christian Writers Fellowship International and is on the staff of the 1991 Arizona Christian Writers Conference.

IF JOHN HAD NOT WRITTEN

Bob Hostetler

But these are written that you may believe that Jesus is the Christ, the Son of God, and that by believing you may have life in his name. (John 20:31, NIV)

The old man hunched in the doorway of his home in Ephesus and stared at the blank papyrus surface spread across his knees. He was remembering the recent argument he'd been having with the young disciple who shared his home.

"Did not Matthew," the old man said, "and Mark and Luke already record such things?"

"But," the young man retorted, "you yourself have told me many things they did not write."

"Yes," he said, "but Jesus did so many things. If they were all written, I suppose the world could not contain the books."

"But," the other said with flaming eyes, "the others were not confronted with the Gnostics as we have been! They did not deal with their lies!"

The aging apostle quieted. He knew the harm the Gnostics had done — and may yet do — in the young church. His friend was right. Another gospel must be written.

That scene, of course, is mostly out of my imagination. But what if John had not written? What if the "beloved disciple" had left the hard job of writing to others?

Would the Gnostic heresy have gained followers? Would the Council of Nicea have yielded tragically different results? Would truth have taken a back seat?

It's impossible to say. But then it's impossible to say what will happen if I don't write, if you don't write. It's impossible to say what message will go unsaid or what person left untouched if Christians whom God has gifted and called to write do not.

Should I forbear because I am old, or tired, or because writing is so hard, or because my first attempts were rejected, or because others seem to have a much greater gift?

The disciple whom Jesus loved probably went through many of the same things. But he wrote, nonetheless. And left a lesson for me.

God, I feel Your touch and I know I'm to ...

Bob Hostetler, a Captain in The Salvation Army, has written for *The War Cry, Writer's Digest, Presbyterian Survey* and dozens of other publications. His first book, a collaboration with Josh McDowell entitled *Don't Myth the Truth When It's Staring You Straight in the Faith*, is scheduled release by Word Books.

VISION *to see*

FAITH *to believe*

COURAGE *to do.*

ELMER LAPPEN

© btn

FIRST THINGS FIRST

Mary Ann Howard

But they that wait upon the Lord shall renew their
strength.   (Isaiah 40:31a, TLB)

"The hurrier I go the behinder I get," is an old
Pennsylvania Dutch saying. It describes exactly how I
react under pressure. Publishers' deadlines, ringing
telephones and houseguests create anguish within me.
Interruption blocks my flow of thoughts.

My husband and I both operate people-oriented
businesses in our home. The resulting responsibilities
and frequent traveling shoves my writing aside. One of
my writing teachers said, "Writing can wait but
relationships can't." However, it's difficult for me to
control unexpected circumstances and master the
problem of time-stealers. I get frustrated sitting in a
pile of books and papers and lose my patience.

Writing is a burn from within, something I must do.
It is emotional therapy and refreshes me. I feel an
urgency to get my message onto the printed page and to
the reader. When I become frustrated and
overwhelmed, I realize I am operating in my own
strength and not the Lord's.

There is only one way I have found to survive a busy

schedule and be a successful writer. God wants pre-eminence in each of our lives. He wants to set our priorities and orchestrate our schedules. He expects to receive the glory and honor for our activities. We must learn to step aside and let Him rule our minutes, hours and days.

My constant prayer is, "Lord, I am yours. Mold me and make me what You want me to be."

Lord Jesus, I am Yours. I pray that You will direct my new approach, which is ...

_____

_____

_____

_____

_____

_____

_____

_____

_____

Mary Ann Howard, of Prescott, Arizona, is a clinical nutritionist, free-lance writer, and author of a book entitled *Blueprint for Health*. She is also a public speaker and the Teaching Director of the Prescott Community Bible Study.

RELEASING THE CREATOR WITHIN

Kevin Hrebik

Whoever believes in me...streams of living water will flow from within him. (John 7:38, NIV)

I have often wondered at the marvel that man is made in God's image. Before salvation, we were only a dim reflection of our Creator. Now we have our Lord — our Creator — living inside us, changing our natures to match His perfect nature.

What does this mean to the writer, someone who in turn attempts to create? God blesses, loves, and inspires us through each other. Just as writers in general have a special gift, different from other gifts of the body of Christ, so each writer is unique among all other writers. Each Christian writer has a special message for the body of Christ and the world, a message from the Creator.

More than ever the world needs Jesus Christ! Yet Christian writers sit with hearts full of the fruits of the spirit — and can't find words! I don't believe a Christian should ever have more than a temporary case of writer's block. Can you imagine Christ in front of a crowd — at a loss for words?

There are many "tricks" to spark the proverbial

"creative juices," but prayer is rarely mentioned as a writer's tool. Yet what else brings us closest to the source of all creativity, and our Creator?

When words don't come, don't panic. To rephrase an old line — words are only a prayer away. After all, they aren't really our words, are they?

Remember, God has something to say to us — through you.
Don't ask what you can say, ask what God has to say.

Father, fill me with Your living water and show me how to say ...

_____

_____

_____

_____

_____

_____

_____

Kevin Hrebik has been a writer for *Cornerstone* magazine; editor of *Channels* -- the magazine of the Christian Writers' League of America; Editorial Director of Abbey Press; and founder of New Leaf Desktop Publishing. In 1988 he started *Living Streams*, a magazine for Christian writers. He has sold many articles and greeting cards and has also taught at writing conferences nationwide.

THE VOICE OF GOD

Rodney Hugen

The voice of the Lord is powerful, the voice of the Lord is full of majesty. (Psalm 29:40, RSV)

"Your bass voice will be perfect," Pastor said. I agreed to take part in the dramatic reading before he added, "We'll be performing a piece about God calling Moses and you'll be the voice of God."

The voice of God! How silly it sounded. Asking me to be the voice of God? Surely he was joking. I thought about how a perfect God would say the words I was given to say. Would He stutter? Would He need to clear His throat?

Performance night arrived and I trembled as I looked out at the congregation. Like Moses, I stammered my way through. After the service, a group of friends teased me about being God's voice. They were right. I didn't feel like I was speaking for Him.

I headed to my car, grateful the night was over. A lady stepped from between cars and said softly, "I heard God speaking through you tonight. I needed to hear His message. I hope you'll always speak so clearly for Him."

I was the voice of God. So are you. When we

speak His Word, He is using our voice as though it were His. Our voices may be weak and inadequate, but His is powerful and full of majesty. Go ahead. Be the voice of God. He wants you to be.

Heavenly Father, use these words to ...

_____

_____

_____

_____

_____

_____

_____

_____

_____

_____

Rodney Hugen is a free-lance writer who also enjoys dramatic reading and narrating. A resident of Phoenix, Arizona, Rodney has been published in his denominational magazine and is a frequent contributor to his church newsletter.

THE PROMISE OF A PAGE

Ellen Humbert

This is the day which the Lord hath made; we will rejoice
and be glad in it.   (Psalms 118:24, KJV)

Picture the day as part of a book that we can help to write.
And day by day, page by page...
the paper smooth and white stretches out before us...
waiting to be filled...
a quiet place, set aside...
a spot on which to build.

For this is a day the Lord has made. Watch, it opens wide...
like a book that calls us...
inviting us inside,
asking us to listen...
asking us to see...
promising a treasure in what the day can be.

Brand-new, beginning...Lord we greet the day,
off'ring what we have to You...
hear us as we pray.
Teach us...encourage us...there's so much to know...
and help us remember it's through Your Love we grow
closer to what each of us can be...
closer to a time when we will see on the page before us,
a way You choose to reach the hungry...the thirsty...

a way You choose to teach the people of the world
a brand-new song...
and Lord, a way to keep the children strong.

It's a brand-new page to write upon...
a page that seems to say...
"Come, share your vision. Come sing your songs today."
It's another chapter in the book...
a setting of the stage...
a journey just beginning in the promise of a page.

Dear Lord, let me share Your vision and sing Your song by ...

_____

_____

_____

_____

_____

_____

_____

_____

_____

Ellen Humbert is a public school teacher of handicapped children
in Mesa, Arizona. Her original songs, poems, children's stories and
devotionals are incorporated into the worship, education and social
activities of the church where she and her husband serve.

FINDING THE FOCUS

Diana L. James

For I know the plans I have for you, says the Lord. They are plans for good and not for evil, to give you a future and a hope.
(Jeremiah 29:11, TLB)

A few years ago I read again the above quote from Jeremiah and wondered: "Does the Lord really have a plan for MY life?" I was running at a frantic pace just to keep from going backwards and kept wondering where the pattern or plan was.

My speaking career was not progressing and my writing career was suffering from the dreaded malady: W.B. (Writer's Block). The line "If God had intended for people to fly, He'd have made it easier to get to the airport" went through my head. I laughed and thought, *If God has a plan for my life, why doesn't He put it where I can find it?*

I began focusing on two-way communication with God, asking Him to lead me and point out the way that I should go. I learned to shut out the perplexity of the world and focus my attention just on Him, submitting my will to His. Suddenly, He began to put positive, constructive, and humorous ideas into my head.

Focusing only on those inspired ideas and giving God credit (and gratitude), I was able to push aside distractions and negative influences that had held me back from being all that God wanted me to be.

The result was, I have discovered new ways to incorporate humor into my speaking career, and God seems to be blessing it every step of the way. Day by day, I know I am doing what God would have me do, and the joy of that assurance is my strength.

I meet Him regularly in order to keep my focus. He has taught me that a speech that's full of sparkling wit will keep the audience grinning, especially if the end of it is close to the beginning. Self-doubt have given way to the confidence I needed. The simple act of focusing on Him taught me to trust His plans — plans to give me a future, with humor and hope.

Holy Father, bless me with confidence to ...

_____

_____

_____

_____

_____

_____

_____

_____

Diana James is a member of the National Speakers Association, recipient of the Silver Microphone Award from that organization, and founder of Southern California Convention Speakers. Her articles have appeared in many national publications. She has had two books published and her work was recently included in an anthology entitled *Marketing Masters.*

HEAVENLY WRITER'S CONFERENCES

Rebecca Barlow Jordan

In the morning, O Lord, Thou wilt hear my voice; in the
morning I will order my prayer to Thee and eagerly watch.
(Psalm 5:3, NAS)

"Where do you get ideas for writing?"

Invariably, that question always arises at writer's conferences. I love those challenging times with other speakers and writers each year. However, the majority of my ideas for writing emerge as a result of another special meeting time. As I meet the Lord each morning in quiet moments of prayer, reflection, and study, He faithfully speaks His thoughts, His personal words for me.

In order to maintain that channel of communication, I must guard that time as the diligent Psalmist guarded His precious sheep. I must watch from His Word expectantly, like a soldier, alert in His lookout place from the watchtower. Enemies such as worry, fear, noise, and deadlines wait to rob me of those quiet, victorious moments and daily, creative opportunities. And some mornings, when I feel as though I have already battled all night with sleeplessness, only an act of my will ushers me into God's presence.

Writer's block rarely defeats me, when I have spent

precious moments alone with Him. As I seek first to know Him intimately, then offer my life as a blank page to the Lord, He fills my file folder full of ideas throughout the day...many of which were born in our heavenly writer's conferences together. "Praise God, from whom all ideas and blessings flow!"

Lord, I hear You saying to me ...

_____

_____

_____

_____

_____

_____

_____

_____

_____

A pastor's wife, **Rebecca Jordan** has sold numerous religious articles and devotionals, over 800 greeting card verses and poems, and wrote a weekly devotional newspaper column for ten years for the *Chandler Arizonan*. She has also taught Bible study classes for all ages, led women's retreats, and currently teaches a Bible study in her women's ministry at their Allen, Texas church.

THE OLD MESSAGE— EVER NEW

Mary Lou Klingler

I am He that liveth, and was dead; and, behold, I am
alive forevermore.   (Revelation 1:18, KJV)

Vainly I searched for a special story as my husband
and I toured Europe. Nothing! I didn't have one idea
that hadn't been written a dozen times before in travel
magazines.

On the last morning we rode the cograil up Mt.
Pilatus to view the world from the top of the Swiss Alps.

As we rode up--up--up, we watched the city of
Lucerne grow smaller and smaller. We passed cabins
that reminded me of "Heidi," one of my favorite
childhood heroines.

We thrilled to the view of snow-clad mountains and
intermittent floating clouds, mountain goats and sheep
grazing in patches of green pasture. The sound of
tinkling cowbells drifted skyward, breaking the awesome
quiet. We strolled around the top of the mountain and
gazed down into the green valley where a little white
church nestled at the base of a hill. On the top of that
hill stood a large wooden cross silhouetted against the
blue sky.

Minutes later we watched heavy clouds roll in and

cover the green pastures and the little church. Everything was enveloped in a frothy white except the cross.

That was it! I'd gone halfway around the world hoping to find a story and there it was — old, yet ever new — the empty cross! Jesus led me to a mountaintop to remind me that he lives — and that's the story that makes the difference.

I returned home with great joy. I had my assignment.

My Lord and Savior, my assignment is ...

_____

_____

_____

_____

_____

_____

_____

Mary Lou Klingler divides her year between Paulding, Ohio and Phoenix, Arizona. She is the founder and co-leader of the Bethany Christian Writers' Club of Phoenix, and has had over 100 published articles, stories and devotionals in such magazines as *Reader's Digest, Decision*, and *Signs of the Times*. Mary Lou also speaks at writers' seminars, church programs, AARP meetings, and Friends of the Library.

JOY, PURE AND SIMPLE

Bev Koski

Then you will find your joy in the Lord, and I will cause you to ride on the heights of the land.

(Isaiah 58:14, NIV)

I'd been sitting at my desk for hours writing an article about joy, shuffling through the pages of random notes that just weren't coming together. I had been concentrating on the above verse, one of my favorites.

I finally decided to stop struggling and go for my daily walk — a valuable tool in my writing. As I walk, I make a concentrated effort to empty my mind of my own thoughts and ask God to share His wisdom with me.

On this particular day God gave me an unforgettable lesson in joy. I'd been walking for several blocks, enjoying the sun's warmth, when suddenly I heard the voice of a young girl behind me.

"Daddy! Daddy! Look how fast I'm going!" she squealed in sheer delight. "Oh, Daddy, I'm flying like an eagle!" I turned around and saw a little girl roller-skating alongside her dad, her face one huge grin! She seemed to be gliding effortlessly, her long blond braids trailing in the wind. Just as the two of them

145

skated past me, she said, "Oh, Daddy, I don't drag you down anymore! Look! I'm flying like an eagle!"

It all clicked into place. "That's it," I said to myself. I don't drag my Father or anyone else down when I have the wings of an eagle, the wings of joy. How I thanked God for showing me a little girl's unadulterated joy!

My Father, let me fly like an eagle and ...

_____

_____

_____

_____

_____

_____

_____

_____

_____

_____

Bev Koski has written Bible studies, church services, devotionals, and inspirational poetry and articles. She also leads Bible studies in her home town of Mesa, Arizona.

THE LORD IS MY EMPLOYER

Muriel Larson

Whatever you do, do it all for the glory of God.
(1 Corinthians 10:31b, NIV)

I have served the Lord as a Christian writer for over thirty years, and I think the reason He has blessed me so greatly in this is because I consider Him my employer, guide, and Lord.

Each morning when I awake I praise my Master and report for duty. This has led to many adventures in His service about which I've been able to write.

The benefits of considering the Lord as my employer are many. For instance, if I didn't, I think I might be crushed when I receive thirteen rejections in one day including two for books! But since He is my employer, He knows just where and when He wants to place those articles and books for His glory, so who am I to question His hand on my work?

Just recently I had a book accepted for publication after 47 rejections in eight years. I rejoiced in the Lord. It was accepted by the best possible publisher for that type of book!

When I first stepped out on faith to support myself and my little girl as a full-time writer, I knew my heavenly Employer would see to all our needs — and He certainly has. If I had chosen instead the steady job offered me, I never would have had 4,500 more articles and 14 more books published.

I believe that if our Lord calls us to write for Him, it is one of the most exciting and challenging opportunities in the world. Just think — He chooses to use us to reach millions for His glory!

Lord God, as my employer, direct my …

_____

_____

_____

_____

_____

_____

_____

_____

_____

Muriel Larson of Greenville, South Carolina has had 17 books and more than 5,000 writings accepted for publication. She has taught at Christian writers conferences and serves as faculty advisor for the writers course given by the Southern Baptist Center for Biblical Studies.

IN ALL
LABOR
THERE
IS
PROFIT,

but mere
talk
leads
only
to
poverty.

PROVERBS 14:23

© btn

LESS IS MORE

Steven R. Laube

*You have too many men for me to deliver Midian into
their hands.* (Judges 7:2, NIV)

Gideon was aghast to hear the Lord ask him to cut
back on his army. Already the odds were stacked
against them with only 32,000 Israelites, opposed to
135,000 Midianites.

The first layoff slashed 68 percent of his forces. The
second cut further reduced his numbers by another 97
percent! To his credit, Gideon never questioned the
wisdom of God's actions. Imagine the thoughts of those
who remained. However, God in His divine sovereignty
had a plan. He wanted the Israelites to learn that it was
not their own strength that would save them. (Judges
7:2)

There is a similar approach in the editorial process
of writing. You have sweated and struggled to find the
proper words to develop your thoughts. To your
profound shock, your editor has asked you to cut a third
of the material and to rewrite another third. Your
anger and frustration begins to slowly burn within you.
At that moment, remember the lesson of Gideon: Less
is More. Too often we find security in excess verbiage.

We are a culture burdened and buried by a barrage of words. The more words we wrap around our message, the less threatened we feel. We then proudly say, "Surely no one can argue with that."

My encouragement to you is to edit, edit, edit. Rewrite, rewrite, rewrite. Let the spirit of God refine your words as He refined Gideon's army. Dwell on the adage that less is more, and you will find yourself conquering the previously unassailable fortress of successful writing.

Dear Jesus, help me refine ...

_____

_____

_____

_____

_____

_____

_____

Steven R. Laube has been in Christian bookselling for the last ten years. He is the national buyer for the Berean Christian bookstore chain, and the general manager at the Phoenix, Arizona Berean Christian Bookstore, which was named the 1989 Christian Bookseller's Association National Store of the Year. His publishing history includes *The Bookstore Journal, Publisher's Weekly*, and *God's Promises for Your Finances.*

TRANSFORMING WORDS

Florence Littauer

*You are our letter, written in our hearts, known and read
by all men; being manifested that you are a letter of
Christ, cared for by us, written, not with ink but with the
Spirit of the living God, not on tablets of stone, but on
tablets of human hearts.* (2 Corinthians 3:2-3, NASB)

A lady once wrote me, "Florence, so much has
happened to me in the past year. It was almost as if
our Father sent me to you in preparation." She told of
many difficult events and then said, "My dear friend lost
a 23-year-old son through suicide. Your book, *Blow
Away the Black Clouds*, helped both of us so much. The
good news you brought me has changed my life. Thank
you for being open and for continuing on with your love
and encouragement."

As writers and speakers we often spend more time
in trying to be cute, clever, and creative than in seeking
God's message that He wishes us to communicate. In
the verses preceding the above text, Paul tells us that
we are personal letters of recommendation, we are
open testimonies to the power of Christ in our lives. As
we write we give out words that are not merely pleasant
thoughts on paper, but are engraved onto the hearts of
our readers.

What an awesome responsibility is ours when we
realize that our message can be used by God to change
lives. Once we accept that it is neither prose nor poetry

but the power of the Holy Spirit that transforms people, we will drop to our knees and plead for God's inspiration that our message would be His words and not merely ours.

May we all be used as open letters of recommendation for the Lord Jesus, offering hope to a troubled world.

Father in heaven, may these experiences ...

_____

_____

_____

_____

_____

_____

_____

_____

Florence Littauer is the president and founder of CLASS Speakers and the author of 19 books. Her writing has been honored with numerous awards and many of her titles have sold over 100,000 copies. A resident of San Marcos, California, Florence has been a guest on TV and radio programs with an average of 100 appearances a year. She also has a daily radio program, "Accent on Life."

THE SECRET PLACE

Elizabeth Long

In thy presence is fullness of joy.
(Psalm 16:11b, KJV)

With only days left before a speaking engagement, I found myself filled with dread, unable to focus on anything I felt would be worthy of the time and attention of an audience. What had happened to me? I had been studying, pondering, and praying, yet nothing seemed to click, until my sister called to talk about her six-year-old grandson.

"Remember how thrilled Cooper was when he got that digital watch he had been wanting for so long?" she asked. "He loved that watch so much, and now he can't find it. You've never seen such a long face on anyone...all his joy is gone." As she related how they had searched the house, the car, and every pocket of his new jacket with no results, I knew my problem. I had lost my joy, but why?

The next few days, like Cooper, I searched my heart and mind trying to find the clue to my problem, with no results until my sister called again.

"Cooper found his watch!" she told me. "He called this morning to tell me that he found it in the secret pocket of his new jacket. No one else knew about that secret pocket, and he had forgotten about it."

That was it! I needed to find that special secret place of fellowship with the Lord once again. Time in His presence, enjoying Him. Then the joy would come. I had my answer and my message.

Father God, what do You want to say to me in our secret place today?

_____

_____

_____

_____

_____

_____

_____

_____

_____

_____

Betty Long is a wife, mother, grandmother, Bible teacher, and speaker for various women's groups. She currently ministers with "Coming Alive in The Spirit," an interdenominational outreach to those with cancer. She lives in Phoenix, Arizona.

YOUR FRUIT SHALL REMAIN

Opal Mabe

*Ye have not chosen me, but I have chosen you, and
ordained you, that ye should go and bring forth fruit, and
that your fruit should remain; that whatever ye shall ask of
the Father in my name, he may give it to you.*

(John 15:16, KJV)

It is said that John Newton's mother prayed for her
wayward son's conversion long after he ran away to sea.
After her death, her prayers were answered and the
former slave trader became the "sailor preacher" of
London, bringing thousands to Christ. His hymn
"Amazing Grace" is today as meaningful as when he
wrote the words which were his testimony of the grace
and forgiveness of God. John Newton's words reached
skeptical Thomas Scott, whose writings later led scores
to Christ, including William Cowper. Cowper's poetry
and prose touched many, one being William
Wilberforce, the British statesman who worked
vigilantly for the abolition of slavery.

There is a stooped and white-haired woman in the
mountains of North Carolina who years ago saw my
need as a troubled young person and quietly invited me
to church. It was the tears on her face, as she played

the piano for the congregation to sing the closing hymn, that caused me to go forward and become converted. Later, as I worked in Child Evangelism, many children accepted Christ. One of these children was my own seven-year-old who grew up to become a tireless teacher of children, leading hundreds to Christ. At least two that prayed the sinner's prayer with her had their lives cut short, a boy on a skateboard on a busy street and a college student who was killed in an accident on the way home from college. When the records were checked at our church, it was found that both had accepted Christ under her ministry. There should be many stars in the crown of Edna Sparks, almost ninety years old, still living in the mountains of North Carolina.

My God and Master, I pray in Jesus' Name for ...

_____

_____

_____

_____

_____

_____

Opal Mabe is a charter member of the Christian Writer's Group of Phoenix. She worked for many years as a teacher and a field representative for Child Evangelism Fellowship, published several articles and three books.

MY STAR

Rosemarie D. Malroy

When they saw the star, they were overjoyed.
(Matthew 2:10, NIV)

Christmas responsibilities smothered me. It had been weeks since I processed a word.

"God help me." I prayed as I turned to the scriptures. I wanted to serve God through writing but sometimes it seemed impossible. Yet in this Christmas story, God gave me hope and set my star shining.

Here the goal of the Wise Men to see the newborn king was embodied in the star. Accomplishing my writing goals is my star.

As the Wise Men lost their star in Jerusalem, I too lose sight of my star — my bright goals. My star or my hope of reaching my writing goals disappears under the cloud of ill health and family responsibilities. Yet I, too, like the Wise Men, must continue my journey.

In Jerusalem they asked the king for directions and went on their way without the benefit of their star. I must do what I can to reach my goals even if it is merely writing a paragraph or checking the markets. I ask God for directions and continue on like the Wise Men. Then my star will also reappear. Finally, like the Wise Men, I will arrive at my goal. Then I can praise God and present Him with my gift — the completion of my writing project.

Gracious Lord, my goals are ...

_____

_____

_____

_____

_____

_____

_____

_____

_____

_____

_____

_____

_____

Rosemary Malroy is the founder and leader of the Fountain Hills, Arizona Christian Writers Club, and the author of three books and several articles.

A PRONOUN IS...

Dr. John L. Mitchell

And my God shall supply all your needs according to His riches in glory in Christ Jesus. (Philippians 4:19, NAS)

Pronouns! I first heard of pronouns in elementary school. The teacher told us that a pronoun was a word used in place of a noun.

She then explained that pronouns come in three persons —"I, you and he." And then there are cases of pronouns —"Me" for "I" and "him" for "he." The teacher added that pronouns could be singular or plural. Of course, there are different genders as well. It was so confusing.

I thought I had heard all there was to know about pronouns. But then in seminary I learned the importance of watching for "possessive pronominal adjectives."

While studying the above verse, I made a new discovery of pronoun significance. Paul uses two possessive pronouns as adjectives — "my" and "your." What's so great about that? Did you notice what each of them modifies? The verse states "my God" and "your needs." Paul did not write that my God would meet my needs. Nor that your God would meet your needs.

Who is "my God?" He is the God who had previously met Paul's needs through the Philippian people. And now, because they had seen that Paul's needs were met, Paul is assuring them that God would meet their needs.

As men and women who prepare written or spoken messages for others, let us remember that our purpose is to meet their needs. And then we can claim the promise that God will supply our needs according to His riches in glory in Christ Jesus.

Beloved Father, my needs are ...

_____

_____

_____

_____

_____

_____

_____

Dr. John L. Mitchell recently retired after 28 years as Pastor of Bethany Bible Church in Phoenix, Arizona. Previously, he was Assistant Pastor of the Church of the Open Door in Los Angeles. Dr. Mitchell currently teaches and serves on the Board of Regents of Dallas Theological Seminary. He has contributed to a theological journal and formerly wrote a column for the *Arizona Republic*, entitled "Point of View."

THE OLDER WOMAN

Linda Montoya

Similarly, the older women must behave in ways that befit those who belong to God...By their good example they must teach the younger women to love their husbands and children. (Titus 2:3-4, NAS)

In my twenties, life was a series of struggles. Being married young, having children, caring for home, worrying about discipline, money, sex, husband and in-laws — everything was a burden.

Other churches in the area offered classes in homemaking skills, parenting and Bible studies. I especially envied those communities where the older women nurtured the young marrieds. They encouraged them. They listened to them. And, most of all, these beautiful seasoned ladies opened up Bibles and shared the wealth spring of power, joy and happiness in God's Word with the new generation of women.

In my parish, however, it seemed that everyone had it all together, at least on the outside. No one talked about emotions or problems. I needed help to deal with the realities of life.

At age 27, I committed this to prayer. I prayed that God would raise up older women in my parish who really knew Him; those who loved and wanted to serve Him. We needed speakers, and discussion groups where we could encourage one another to become women of excellence, strength and inner beauty that comes from a relationship with Jesus Christ.

For four years I prayed. Then I heard an inner voice, as if the Lord was saying, "Well, Linda, you're older now!"

God was calling me to serve at my church. I knew that our two priests couldn't possibly begin to meet all the spiritual needs of 6500 parishioners. Certainly many lay people would have to be willing to serve.

In saying "Yes" to the Lord, I realized that although I had been willing to use my strengths and talents in service before, this was the first time I had ever allowed God to use my greatest weakness. You see, I was terrified to speak in front of other people.

In offering the Lord my weakness, I have tasted the joy of ministering to thousands of people through the spoken and written word.

Loving God, let me taste the joy of ministering by ...

_____

_____

_____

_____

Linda Montoya, formerly with Evergreen Communication, Inc., has spoken to many groups and has received several awards for public speaking. She has also been published in numerous magazines including *Guideposts* and *Focus on the Family.* She lives in Ventura, California.

Our doubts are traitors
and make us lose
the good we oft
might win by fearing to

ATTEMPT

William Shakespeare

©ktn

IS THE PUMP RUSTY?

Kathleen A. O'Day

Guard my words as your most precious possession. Write them down, and also keep them deep within your heart.
(Proverbs 7:2,3, TLB)

I could see the radiating purple, pink, and golden hues above the homes to the east. It was always my first gift from God each morning as I peeked out the window from my hospital bed. I felt warmed by His presence. Everyday He changed it a little bit, adding fiery reds and sometimes softer beige and bluish tones.

Today as I glanced out over the colored hues in the sky, I wanted to pick up my pen and write. I've always loved to share with others, to comfort them, and to offer them hope. It was another one of the gifts from God that he had freely given, but I had pushed it aside for three and one-half years now. The pump was pretty rusty. Could it be primed, I wondered. It was time to find out.

Writing out a small devotional was a beginning. In it I shared that God chooses what we go through in life, even when we suffer and how we suffer, but we choose how we go through it. It felt great sharing through my pen what God has taught me. I may be a little rusty, but the pump's not broken.

God calls us to write His words and keep them deep within our hearts, so that we might keep encouraging others to come to know His everlasting grace, His mercy, and His forgiveness. Through Him, we are able to experience the love and fellowship of Christ and his people.

O healing Christ, thank you for priming my pump so I may ...

_____

_____

_____

_____

_____

_____

_____

_____

_____

Kathleen O'Day has had several devotionals published and worked on the staff of a Christian newspaper. She also has spoken to groups in the Phoenix, Arizona area. Kathleen suffers from a chronic illness.

WORDS

Janette Oke

*Let the words of my mouth, and the meditation of my
heart, be acceptable in Thy sight, O Lord, my strength,
and my redeemer.* (Psalm 19:14, KJV)

I was amazed as I glanced through my Bible
concordance to see how often Scripture speaks of
"words." It talks of the sweetness of words and the
wisdom of words. It mentions gracious words, idle
words, good words, and fit words. It warns of the
danger of hasty or careless words. It speaks of God's
message to man as The Word and refers many times to
the Son as the Living Word.

Words are our medium of communication. They
communicate who we are and what we think, feel, and
believe. Words build up and tear down. Words
encourage and deride. Words can sow love or hatred.
Words can bring laughter or tears.

Perhaps the prayer in the text above could be
breathed each time we sit down to our typewriter or
word processor. Lord, let the words that fill the pages
carry a message to the reader — perhaps many
readers — and bring glory to Him and growth to
another. We need God's help in our writing.

All who write with the English language have the
same storehouse of words. We select from among them
and shape our work to present our chosen message. No
writer has more, or less, "tools" than you have — or
than I have. How we use those tools is what really
counts. May they be "acceptable." May they minister to
others.

Gracious Lord Jesus, let the wisdom of Your Word communicate ...

_____

_____

_____

_____

_____

_____

_____

_____

_____

_____

_____

_____

Janette Oke is the author of nineteen Christian fiction books published by Bethany House Publishers and twelve books for children published by Bethel Publishing. She resides in Canada.

THE LORD'S LEADING

Norman R. Oke

Teach me thy way, O Lord, and lead me in a plain path.
(Psalm 27:11, KJV)

No one knows how old David was when he wrote this Psalm. But regardless of his age, he readily admitted that he needed the leading of the Lord. This is true also with Christian writers and we are wise to recognize it.

In our natural life we can become self-reliant in things we do everyday. They become second nature. And in our writing life, after we've become published, we may also begin to rely on our own talents. So it pays, whether we have been writers for ten, twenty, or more years, to pray as did David, "Lead me in a plain path."

Satan is on the lookout for writers who have become too self-reliant, and we are good objects for his suggestion that we are old enough now to go our way alone. How wise it is for us all, new writers and old-timers as well, to plead daily that He may lead us in our writing so we may touch others.

The significant message of this Psalm is this: No matter how old we are or how long we have written, we still need to be led. And, along with asking the Lord to lead us in a plain path and teach us His way, we can also pray, "Lord, help us write plainly so that we may teach others Thy way."

Good Shepherd, lead me ...

_____

_____

_____

_____

_____

_____

_____

_____

_____

_____

Norman R. Oke is the author of several books and many articles. A former pastor and evangelist, he served as Book Editor for the Nazarene Publishing House and Registrar of Nazarene Bible College, located in Colorado Springs, Colorado, where he now lives. He has also spoken at writers' conferences.

THIS MATTER OF PUBLIC SPEAKING

Dorothy M. Page

Let the words of my mouth and the meditation of my heart be acceptable in thy sight, O Lord, my rock and my redeemer. (Psalm 19:14, RSV)

At one time I was painfully self-conscious. Public speaking threw me into absolute panic. The exact period of my metamorphosis is vague, but somewhere along the way I started to pray about this problem.

I asked the Lord to help me forget about myself and concentrate on the topic. It worked. Since that time I always pray before speaking. It helps me to be totally absorbed by the subject and forget self.

I am convinced that through continuing prayer I have been enabled to present successful programs. Some of them have been published. The positive response of audiences is gratifying, but the greatest reward is knowing that my Lord is in charge.

Almighty God, I pray that You take charge of ...

_____

_____

_____

_____

_____

_____

_____

_____

_____

_____

_____

Dorothy M. Page wrote a newspaper column under her byline, published poetry, drama, and short stories. She presents programs incorporating music, commentary, and color slides, and has also served as program coordinator for both youth and adult groups. She lives in Sun City, Arizona.

HIS WORDS

Birdie Etchison Perry

*In the beginning was the Word, and the Word was with
God, and the Word was God.* (John 1:1, NKJV)

Each time I sit in front of my typewriter, a mental
picture flashes through my mind. Words. I'm soon
going to put words on paper. Words that will become
sentences, paragraphs, pages, and possibly chapters,
depending on what project I choose to work on.

I think of Eliza Doolittle in *My Fair Lady* and her
exclaiming, "Words, words, words! All I hear is words!"
Yes, words are what make a story, a poem, a play, a
book. And need I add that I am utterly enchanted,
enthralled, enamored with words?

When reading, I often ask myself, "What if the
author had constructed the sentence another way?
Would this passage be more effective?" And that is
what writers must be aware of: making our words form
patterns, making certain they portray pictures so the
reader must use his senses.

The New King James version of John 1:1 is one of
my favorite verses to think about as I sit pondering
about what I will say on this particular day.

There is something about that phrase, "In the
beginning" that makes me pause and think. In the
beginning this idea was good, but will it work? Will it
say what I want it to? What I say will be read by others
for inspiration, for insight, for enlightenment. My

prayer is that my words will come from God, the Maker of all things on this earth.

Lord, let this be the beginning of ...

_____

_____

_____

_____

_____

_____

_____

_____

_____

_____

_____

Birdie Etchison Perry is President of the Willapa Writer's Circle on Long Beach Peninsula, Washington, where she writes full time. She has had five books published and has sold to more than ninety publications. Birdie is also an instructor for the Writer's Digest Fiction Course.

INTRUSIONS

Joan Podlewski

I am restless in my complaint and am surely distracted.
(Psalm 55:2, KJV)

Juggling a writing career and raising a family has its frustrations as well as joys.

Some days the phone seems to ring constantly because I want to write undisturbed. An appointment with the orthodontist is scheduled just when the creative juices began to flow. Hubby comes home unexpectedly for lunch and I must stop writing to keep him company while he eats. At other times distraction comes in the form of the latest issue of a writer's magazine, a friend's invitation to lunch, or a request to bake cookies for the PTA meeting.

It is easy to let resentment build up when the demands of family and friends intrude upon our precious writing time. However, our attitude toward these intrusions is important. We can choose to act irritable and become frustrated over them or we can respond in a loving manner to each one who comes to us with a special need.

Choosing the proper attitude toward distractions will enable us to become better writers. Frustration, complaining, and restlessness deplete the creative energy writing requires.

The strange thing is, since I've begun practicing this principle, I'm writing more than ever.

Jesus, fill me with an attitude of joy toward ...

_____

_____

_____

_____

_____

_____

_____

_____

_____

_____

_____

_____

Joan Podlewski is the Women's Minister on the pastoral staff of Trinity Wesleyan Church in Jackson, Michigan. She founded and led the Christian Writers Group in Jackson, and has been published in several magazines including *Good Housekeeping.*

NO OTHER GODS

Jan Potter

You shall have no other gods before Me.
(Exodus 20:3, KJV)
...You shall love the Lord your God with all your heart, and with all your soul, and with all your mind...You shall love your neighbor as yourself. (Matthew 22:37-39,NASB)

"What?! Give up writing? You've got to be kidding!" I glared at my husband in disbelief. But the look on his face told me he wasn't joking. Rick had asked me not to write any more and not even to talk about writing.

I went to my bedroom, locked the door, and dropped to my knees by my bed.

"Why?" I implored God. "How could Rick ask me to give up something so important to me?" The answer came quickly and clearly as the Lord spoke the words to my mind.

Because you've made writing an idol.

An idol? At first I disagreed. I didn't worship writing or pray to writing.

Admittedly, article ideas woke me each morning, book themes occupied my daytime thinking, short story imaginings lulled me to sleep at night, and poetry lyrics danced through my dreams. But an idol?

As I thought about it, I had to face the fact. Even though this writing business was relatively new to me and I hadn't yet been published, I could see that it had become an obsession. It was a priority over God and my family. How often, I thought, I had ignored my children and been only half attentive to their needs because of my preoccupation.

And now I was asked to give it up.

"OK, Lord, I surrender," I prayed. I'll give up writing if that's what you want."

It took a deliberate act of my will to replace thoughts of writing with thoughts of God. While showering in the morning, instead of conjuring up some plot, I chose to sing praises to God, to commit my day to Him. I purposely spent my first available time in the day reading His Word. It didn't come naturally, I had to choose.

Gradually, I could sense God giving back that activity I loved, but not as my first love.

After praying about it together, Rick and I agreed that I should attend a Christian Writer's Conference at Mt. Hermon. At the conference, I sold my first article.

Several years have passed, and the Lord continually reminds me that writing is a gift, calling, a blessing from God, but it must not become a god. I need to keep Him first in my affection and attention.

I'm also aware that God can minister to many people through my writing, making it a vehicle for His love, but I still need to turn off the typewriter when it's time to cook dinner!

Jan Potter's work has appeared in several publications, including *Moody Monthly, Discipleship Journal, Today's Christian Woman* and *Virtue.* She is currently writing a teen morality book series. A resident of Phoenix, Arizona, Jan also speaks at women's retreats.

shall Love the Lord my God with all of my heart with all of my soul with all of my mind with all of my strength.

©LEIGH KNOWLES

MARK 12:30

SHARING THE ADVENTURE

Sue Raatjes

Let the heavens be glad, and let the earth rejoice...Then all the trees of the forest will sing for joy before the Lord, for He is coming. (Psalm 96:11-13, KJV)

Picture yourself as a child, picking your way along a path in a friendly forest. Hundreds of trees stretch their branches to the sun while clumps of violets and buttercups beckon you deeper into the woods. If you spread apart some of the thick undergrowth, you may spot a stately purple and green Jack-in-the-Pulpit.

As a child I loved the woods; its spontaneity delighted me. I never knew what lay in the path through the trees: a clearing of tall grasses and milkweed pods; a blackberry bush ripe with juicy berries; or rocks arranged in a circle, outlining charred ground that once housed a campfire.

"Sh-h-h. What's that noise! The grass is moving..a snake!" Everything inside of me dreaded seeing a snake on my woodsy jaunts, yet I always went. Even that fear made the adventure worthwhile.

As a writer, I can show others that a walk with Jesus is an adventure filled with surprises. There are tough choices to contemplate, serendipities to relish, setbacks to overcome and marvelous growth to measure.

I owe it to my readers to clearly describe not only the delicate buttercups and violets, but also the vexing poison ivy and yes, even the ominous snake in the path. If I keep them in suspense, revealing slowly the surprises along the way, they will follow me closely into the woods of Christian faith. What an adventure to share!

Lord Jesus, I can share my love of You best with others by ...

Sue Raatjes resides in Phoenix, Arizona where she teaches high school English. Her areas of service include Christian Education and free-lance writing. She's written for *Today's Christian Woman, The Upper Room, The Church Herald*, and *Family Life Today*, and has co-authored a book entitled *My Joy Came in the Morning*.

PURE GOLD

Frank Rodocker

But he knoweth the way that I take, when he hath tried
me, I shall come forth as gold. (Job 23:10, KJV)

I have never "tried" gold to remove the impurities.
But it was once part of my job on a small weekly
newspaper in Ohio to sweep up Linotype slugs,
dropped type, and scrap lead, along with dirt, bits of
paper, and cigarette butts, and dump it all in the pot to
melt. Then I skimmed off the dross till the molten lead
was bright like quicksilver, and poured it into new
ingots for a new edition. That's what "tried" means.

When the fires of frustration are the hottest, the
trash is being incinerated and skimmed from our spirits.
After the purifying comes the molding into new forms,
new shapes, new words.

Job's remark begins with, "But..." and follows his
lamentation that he can't seem to find God. What a
glorious revelation for the tired writer! "I don't know
where to turn." Job cries, "but I'm not lost because He
knows where I am going. And after He has purified
me, I'll come forth as gold."

Father, I can feel You molding me into...

_____

_____

_____

_____

_____

_____

_____

_____

_____

_____

_____

_____

Frank Rodocker is currently Vice President of the Arizona State Poetry Society and editor of the Phoenix chapter's newsletter. A retired teacher of English, creative writing, and science fiction, he has written an unpublished novel, numerous plays, and short stories, in addition to two books of poetry. He lives in Glendale, Arizona.

SILENT SEASON

Peggy Romanoski

There is a time for everything, and a season for every activity under heaven: ...a time to be silent and a time to speak. (Ecclesiastes 3:1,7b, NIV)

Communication has always been a priority for me. I wrote my first "novel" at age ten, was editor of the high school paper, and began writing for newspapers in college.

But there came a time when I couldn't write. I thought I would never write creatively again, and for many years I didn't.

Eventually, I experienced a craving to know God better than I knew anyone else. I sensed Him urging, "Write to Me." So I began journaling — letters to Him. Although I envisioned insightful entries, instead they seemed mundane and unspiritual.

But later as I reread them, I found Isaiah 45:3 descriptive: "I will give you the treasures of darkness, riches stored in secret places, so that you may know that I am the Lord, the God of Israel, who summons you by name." (NIV)

My musings, mined from dark times in my life, were studded with insights!

Soon ideas for devotionals, articles, and fiction tumbled through my thoughts. I had to write. And I discovered that during my silent season, God had matured me from a slapdash writer to one with patience to polish.

I no longer fret over periodic times of silence, as I know they are preparation for times to speak. Like the Psalmist, I've discovered, "As for God, His way is perfect." (Psalm 18:30a, KJV)

Heavenly Father, I sense now is the time ...

_____

_____

_____

_____

_____

_____

_____

_____

_____

_____

Peggy Romanoski writes for a local newspaper, contributes regularly to various devotional periodicals, and has been published in *Decision, The Christian Communicator,* and several other religious publications. She is also a speaker for women's groups and is a social worker at a hospice. She lives in Las Vegas, Nevada.

WRITING THROUGH THE HURTS

Melody Rondeau

Praise be to the God and Father of our Lord Jesus Christ, the Father of compassion and the God of all our troubles, so that we can comfort those in any trouble with the comfort we ourselves have received from God.

(2 Corinthians 1:3-4, NIV)

How can I be expected to write encouraging things to help other people when I'm in the pits of depression and can't even help myself? Why do we have to hurt? It gets in the way of creativity. It sidetracks inspiration.

Have you ever felt that way? Disappointments about your circumstances, worry over your finances, or depression because of marital problems — these emotions can all interfere with your writing.

Can any good come out of the low places of our life? Yes, God can use these times. Write about your hurts and disappointments, the painful, the embarrassing times. Suffering makes us real people. Hurting makes us stronger Christians, deeper people, and better writers. It helps our readers identify with us. They need to see that their pain is also felt by another human being.

Write about the good times as well. Record your

feelings of relief from those hard times, your hopes, your answered prayers and victories. Let people see how God can work in our daily lives.

Dear Lord, let me remember the good times and ...

_____

_____

_____

_____

_____

_____

_____

_____

_____

_____

_____

Melody Rondeau lives in Flagstaff, Arizona, where she works part-time at Northern Arizona University, takes classes, and is secretary for her contractor husband. She is currently the main speaker for the MOPS (Mothers of Preschoolers) group in Flagstaff, has taught workshops at women's retreats, and published in *Power for Living, The Flagstaff Woman*, and *Moody Monthly*.

IN HIS TIME

Bonnie Sanders

*If I speak in the tongue of men and of angels, but have
not love, I am only a resounding gong or a clanging
symbol.* (1 Corinthians 13:1, NIV)

The seed, planted by God and nourished by friends,
sprouted and burst into full bloom when watered by a
personal prophecy spoken at my church, "God has
called you to a ministry of writing."

Assuming that meant "instant success," I submitted
manuscripts with confidence. They were all rejected!
What a rude awakening to discover editors couldn't
hear God!

I joined a writer's book club, took a course in
creative writing, and attended writer's conferences. I
cowered in my chair as one instructor admonished,
"Now, don't tell us God called you to write."

A year later I boldly approached an editor at
another seminar. It nearly blew me away when she
said, "If you want your story told, why don't you have
someone else write it?"

But I persevered. One day an editor responded to
my letter that I had something worth saying.

"No, you don't," he wrote, "but God might. You still

have it your agenda more than His. He wants you out of the way so His spirit can work through you."

When I finished pouting I heard the Lord ask, "Are you willing to pay the price?"

I was willing, and through the years, I have found this means allowing His love to flow through me and out to others by submitting to His training, purpose, and timing. Anything less and I'm no more than a resounding gong or a clanging symbol.

Holy Father, I hear You calling me to a ministry of ...

_____

_____

_____

_____

_____

_____

_____

_____

_____

Bonnie Sanders' articles and poetry have appeared in several publications, including *Standard, Sunshine Magazine*, and *Pentecostal Evangel*. She formerly wrote a weekly devotional for her church bulletin. Bonnie resides in Phoenix, Arizona.

WHOSE GIFT? WHOSE CHOICE?

Mildred Schell

You did not choose me, but I chose you, and appointed you, that you should go and bear fruit, and that your fruit should remain. (John 15:16, KJV)

Once I believed that everybody could write, if they only would. Then a perceptive professor asked me to help fellow students in a composition class with their writing. I soon learned that while nearly all can write more clearly and more correctly if they will make the effort, it is true there are some who have a definite gift for the use of words and others who missed that talent entirely.

Eyes twinkling, my friendly professor then "laid it on me": "If you have the gift, you also have a responsibility to use it well." I accepted the fact that I was one with a gift, one who had been chosen.

There are times, however, when I sit at the typewriter and stare at blank paper. Or when I search through ideas I once thought were superior which now seem hopeless. In short, my gift is blocked. But the Giver of the gift, the One Who has chosen me, is readily available. When I seek Him, I see more clearly my responsibility, and the creative juices begin to flow. I am able to bring forth fruit, which shall remain long after I am gone from this earth.

O Lord, You have given me a gift, therefore I must ...

_____

_____

_____

_____

_____

_____

_____

_____

_____

Mildred Schell, a published writer for more than 40 years, has written children's books, poetry, audio-visual resources, curriculum materials, hymn texts, and meditations. A resident of Dayton, Ohio, she is also a speaker and teacher in the field of Christian education.

THE MIRACLE OF PRAYER

Lee Simmons

Have no anxiety about anything, but in everything by prayer and supplication with thanksgiving let your requests be made known to God.   (Philippians 4:6, RSV)

"So you want to be a writer," my high school journalism teacher said, smiling. "Well, we'll see what we can do about that."

I did want to write. How wonderful to be able to put into words the stories and poems running around in my head. Through high school and university I took writing courses, but wasn't satisfied with what I did. I published a few things; I won a few prizes, but it didn't fulfill my inner desire.

I was at my best when writing verse, and gradually I realized this was what I wanted to do. Light verse came easily: Jingles for my friends, poems for greeting cards, lyrics to songs. Still I wasn't satisfied.

One morning during my devotions, I asked God for guidance. And suddenly there it was...I could write inspirational verse, words to His glory, praising Him in rhyme. I thought, "How could I have dared to pray for such a trivial thing?" But I started, and have never stopped.

The miracle of prayer! Each time I sit down to write, I talk to the Lord, and He gives me the right words. I do not pray formally; I simply talk to Him all through the day. He's my friend, and no request is too small. I just say, "Lord, this one is too tough for me; I need Your help."

He furnishes the words to praise His name. He's the best writing teacher I've ever had.

My Lord and Savior, as we talk today, Your help is needed for ...

Lee Simmons has been published by Standard Publishing and Salesian Missions. She divides her time between Mesa and Payson, Arizona where she gives inspirational poetry programs at various churches, clubs, and organizations, and serves as a workshop leader. Her main interest outside of writing is barbershop singing.

THE MINISTRY OF INTERRUPTIONS

Harold Ivan Smith

*Then Simon Peter, who had a sword, drew it and struck
the high priest's servant, cutting off his right ear. The
servant's name was Malchus.*   (John 18:10, KJV)
*But Jesus answered, "No more of this!" And he touched
the man's ear and healed him.*   (Luke 22:51, KJV)

Jesus was on His way to the cross. The cup He had
prayed would pass was not His destiny. Naturally, He
turned to the friends He had cultivated for three years.
The three closest to Him slept while he sweat drops of
blood.

Soldiers approached. Peter attempted to give one
of them a haircut of sorts. Perhaps not fully awake,
instead he amputated the man's ear. Peter's use of
force must have further wounded Jesus.

Jesus stepped forward and restored Malchus' ear.
Clearly a miracle. Yet, one last effort by Jesus to
demonstrate love.

But also a powerful illustration for writers —
particularly those who define their writing as "my
ministry." Sometimes we must drop what we are doing
to help others. Writers, after disciplining their time,
cannot ignore the needs of others. Jesus chose to put
aside His anguish to eliminate the agony of Malchus.

The great German writer, Dietrich Bonhoeffer,

warned us about interruptions — that we must develop a positive reaction rather than an "Oh, no, I don't have time for him..." It's tempting to erect "No Trespassing" signs on the door to our studies and our hearts. But sometimes, Bonhoeffer suggests, God sends the interrupter to help us take a breather or to avoid an error. Occasionally, we return to our typewriter with a fresh perspective — a new insight.

The interruption is not our fault — but our response to that interruption is a decision. If we snarl and growl at every interruption and interrupter, our writing isn't a ministry — it's an obsession.

Lord God, thank you for my fresh perspective on ...

_____

_____

_____

_____

_____

_____

_____

Harold Ivan Smith is the author of more than 20 books. He lives in Kansas City, Missouri, where he serves as President of Harold Ivan Smith and Associates, a consulting firm devoted to the issues of the single adult in the workplace. He is currently doing extensive research on death anxiety among young adults.

THE
LAW
OF
INERTIA

Marie Stewart

Let us not be weary in well doing; for in due season we
shall reap, if we faint not.   (Galatians 6:9, KJV)

The law of inertia has recently commanded my full
attention. Webster defines inertia as the tendency of
matter "when at rest to remain so, and when in motion
to continue moving in a straight line."

As I dieted recently to take off some unwanted
pounds, I found this principle in force. As long as I
continued to deny myself some forbidden delicacy, I felt
little desire for it. But when I indulged just once, the
desire for another — then another — grew!

As writers we know we must write every day to keep
the pump primed. Every day that I don't write, the
inertia sets in more firmly. But if I write something
each day, and continue to write, eventually I have a
finished piece which is marketable.

My desire is to write for the glory of the Lord.
Peter, in his second epistle, admonishes us to add to our

faith "Perseverance" (1:6). God hasn't called me to be successful, but He does require that I be faithful, day after day.

Dear Jesus, Your word teaches me to ...

_____

_____

_____

_____

_____

_____

_____

_____

_____

_____

_____

Marie Stewart is a free-lance writer and teacher of two weekly interdenominational Bible study classes in Glendale, Arizona. She has had over 75 articles and poems published, and reprints have appeared in 60 additional publications.

LETTING GO

Sally E. Stuart

And ye shall know the truth, and the truth shall make you free. (John 8:32, KJV)

Several years ago, I wrote my first book with a go-ahead from an editor. It took six months of writing and a grueling two weeks of almost constant typing to finish the final draft. The editor was waiting impatiently.

During those months, as I came up against each obstacle, I prayed, "Lord, this is your book — help make it the best it can be." Each time He faithfully pushed me over the hump.

By the time it was ready to mail, I was totally exhausted. As I closed the box, a little voice inside me said, "Don't send it." I tried to ignore it, but it persisted. Surely it was Satan trying to keep my masterpiece from a waiting world.

I sealed the package, dropped it in the mailbox, and was sick to my stomach for three days. Two months later I watched the mailman carry a box to my door. I knew it contained the manuscript — I'd been waiting for it.

The words in the rejection letter weren't important. I sat down with the box and cried. In my heart I'd known all along — it was God's still, small voice I'd ignored. It wasn't that He didn't want it published — its ultimate success proves that. All He wanted was for me to give it to Him — to take my hands off it. I had refused.

From that moment, not only that manuscript, but each one has belonged to Him. It is my job to write them. What happens to them after that is in His hands.

Father God, I work for You. Allow this truth to sink into my heart that I might ...

_____

_____

_____

_____

_____

_____

_____

_____

_____

_____

Sally Stuart has been writing for 22 years, speaking for 17, and has been a full-time free-lancer for the last several. She is the author of 17 books, including the annual *Christian Writer's Market Guide*. She lives in Aloha, Oregon.

A
QUICK
EAR

Susan Talbot

But let everyone be quick to hear, slow to speak.
(James 1:19, NAS)

Nothing worked! Adjectives and adverbs blared their horns at "to be" intersections. Outlined points fender-bendered, paragraphs rear-ended. My traffic-jammed manuscript screeched to a halt and I flicked off the typewriter, exasperated. My preschooler waved her crayoned picture in my face, jolting me back to reality. "Mommy, I've been trying to show you..."

"I'm sorry. Mommy wasn't listening."

"I know!" She rolled her eyes, sighing then grinned and wagged her forefinger at me.

James urges his readers to "be quick to hear, slow to speak." Writers specialize in "speaking," dabbing words on paper like artists, reveling in their creations. But "speakers" must first of all be listeners.

"Quick to hear" primarily involves reception of God's Word. (James 1:21) We're satisfied to swallow some verses with a gulp of prayer, like vitamin pills with morning coffee. But spiritual food is digested through study, meditation and obedience. "One who looks intently at the perfect law...and abides by it, not having

203

become a forgetful hearer but an effectual doer, this man shall be blessed in what he does." (James 1:25)

"Quick to hear" also requires sensitivity to others. A clacking typewriter can drown out a child's giggle, a spouse's sigh, or a friend's invitation. Allow for interruptions! Writers out-of-touch with tears or laughter in their living rooms will never evoke tears or laughter from their readers.

"Quick to hear, slow to speak" implies communication drawn from Biblical knowledge, application, and experience. Effective writers soak in before wringing out words.

Father in heaven, my listening has revealed ...

_____

_____

_____

_____

_____

_____

_____

_____

Susan Talbot lives in Seattle, Washington where she works as a coordinator, editor, and staff writer of a homeschool curriculum project for Alta Vista College. She has been published in *Virtue*.

REALITY CHECK

David R. Talbott

Better is open rebuke/Than love that is concealed.
Faithful are the wounds of a friend/But deceitful are the
kisses of any enemy.   (Proverbs 27:5-6, NAS)

A colleague I've come to love and trust has taught me the wisdom of this proverb. A friend will tell me the truth in love. An immature or untrue friend may conceal needed rebuke, and he's done me no favor. Wounds may hurt, but they'll heal. A non-friend's flattery doesn't help.

Occasionally my friend comes to my office, closes the door and asks, "Got time to give me a reality check?" He'll state a situation and ask for my feedback. "Am I sensing the real problem?" he'll ask. "Is my response logical? Have I missed something obvious? Go ahead...be honest!"

My response often seems inadequate. But he always appreciates my input. Just stating his problem gives him fresh perspective.

It's tougher the other way around. Our roles are reversed when my friend is bold enough to ask, "Do you need a reality check?" His ability to perceive that need in me has grown as our friendship has deepened. I'm often too bashful or proud to ask for help.

There's a direct relationship between my emotional and spiritual health and the effectiveness of my writing and speaking. I need the "wounds of a faithful friend."

As I recover from my wounds and become stronger, the easier it is to hear the input from the Ultimate Reality Check, the Spirit of God, and the better my writing reflects truth and reality.

Thanks, Lord, for reality checks.

My God and Master, Your input has changed my perspective about ...

_____

_____

_____

_____

_____

_____

_____

_____

_____

David R. Talbott is Director of Public Affairs and Resident Musician at the Mount Hermon Christian Conference Center, Mount Hermon, California. He does most of Mount Hermon's institutional writing and editing and is in much demand as a concert pianist and as a conference host and emcee.

THE LOOK THAT SAVES AND IGNITES

Paul P. Tell, Jr.

*I sought the Lord, and he answered me; he delivered me
from all my fears.*   (Psalm 34:4, NIV)

Another rejection slip! What's wrong with me?
This manuscript looked so good when I wrote it, even
better after I polished and sent it off. Now, I'm not so
sure. Maybe it's just another ordinary story. Maybe it's
not up to professional standards and I'm making a fool
of myself sending out amateur work.

How can I stop my self-doubt and feeling of
embarrassment that brings up waves of heat, even
though no one is around?

I really love God and trust that He cares for me
through Jesus, His Son. Can He be disappointed? I
know that I am. I'd like to see more fruit. Time is
slipping by and I don't like looking back over old
notebooks. In my own handwriting they contain
wonderful high thoughts, filled with faith and aspiration
— dreams of doing significant things with eternal value.
But life here is so human, so consumed by small cycles
of details that take time, repeating again and again.

Stop it, Paul! Stop looking at yourself adrift on a
troubled sea — you're sinking in it. So what's a

rejection? How many books or articles can one publisher handle? Even a big one?

Psalm 34:5 tells me, "Those who look to him are radiant; their faces are never covered with shame." It tells me about a face lit up from looking up, a face not covered with shame, but ignited by the eye contact. By looking to Him, the eyes of my spirit and God-given creativity will come to life as I reflect His radiance.

Gracious Lord, I am releasing ...

_____

_____

_____

_____

_____

_____

_____

_____

_____

Paul Tell writes from classroom and business experience. He is the author of a collection of Aesop's Fables in a read-and-reflect book, and enjoys working with groups, asking questions that help each person feel like an explorer. He lives in Akron, Ohio.

GOD GIVES ME HOPE

Carol Joy Thompson

Happy is he...whose hope is in the Lord, his God.
(Psalm 146:5, KJV)

For two years I worked intensely on a book manuscript. My emotions swayed like a kite in the wind; soaring up and away, then plunging in despair. Doubts plagues my mind. I felt so inadequate. I would stare at the passage and ask, *Is the message there? Does it sing? Oh, Lord, will I ever be a writer?*

More than once, when HOPE faded and I considered giving up, my fingers would suddenly move..."inspired." The story would come to life and sparkle as better and brighter words appeared on the screen. They didn't come from me! Laughing like a little kid I squealed with delight..."Isn't that just like my Lord!"

His unfailing care inspires me to pursue this task of writing. No need to shudder and fear, I tell myself. Though I struggle and toil, I'm learning it takes time to free the writer within.

When I am searching for just the right words, I find a wealth of treasure and resource deep inside where HOPE is born. Then I know, as He holds my hand, the future is bright and I can persevere.

Writing is a labor of love! Hard work, yes, but what a channel. A channel to bring a message of HOPE to someone who feels HOPEless...everyone does at some time. For the Christian, HOPE equals confidence — God-confidence. I need that kind of HOPE.

I'll trust this One who leads me, that He can use my willing heart — and fingers — to bring HOPE to others. How can I lose? My HOPE is in the Lord.

Beloved Father, I'm learning to take time to ...

Fifteen years as church secretary, writing for and teaching young women's Bible classes, spurred **Carol Thompson** to step out into the writing field. She recently published her first article for *Advance*, and is currently working on a book. She lives in Apple Valley, California.

GOD'S CALL

As Jesus went on from there, he saw a man named
Matthew sitting at the tax collector's booth. "Follow me,"
he told him, and Matthew got up and followed him.
(Matthew 9:9, NIV)

The most unlikely candidate for the office of apostle
was the tax collector, Matthew. The hatred of the Jews
for the tax collectors was violent, fueled by their
religious conviction that God alone — not Augustus
Caesar — was King.

When Matthew followed Jesus without hesitation,
he paid a unique price. The other disciples who were
fishermen could return to their nets, but when Matthew
left his tax office, he could never go back to this
lucrative business.

Matthew took only one thing with him — his pen, or
more precisely, his skill at writing and keeping records.
Ultimately, he used that talent to compose the most
quoted Gospel in Christian literature.

Mark and Luke referred to him as Levi, but he
called himself Matthew which means "gift of Yahweh."
You may also feel you're an unlikely candidate but if
you accept the challenge of Christ to use your pen for
Him, you, too, can become a "gift of God."

The results of your pen can be permanent. Many of
the stories, articles, and books that you write will be
here long after you are gone. Your words can influence

people, persuade them to change their lives, help them to gain understanding as Matthew's words have done. More importantly, perhaps something you write will lead someone to Christ.

Creator God, let me use my gift from You to ...

_____

_____

_____

_____

_____

_____

_____

_____

_____

_____

_____

Susan Titus is the Associate Director of Biola Writers Institute, a publisher's consultant, and a nationwide speaker. She is also the author of eight books, numerous children's stories, and curriculum materials. She resides in Fullerton, California.

TO DECLARE HIS FAITHFULNESS

Irene Van Liew

I will keep on expecting you to help me. I praise you more and more. I cannot count the times when you have faithfully rescued me from danger. I will tell everyone how good you are, and of your constant daily care.

(Psalms 71:14,15, TLB)

Many times my family has heard me say, "Someday I'm going to write."

During the past thirty-two years, my days have been spent being Mom to eight children. While ideas for writing were bountiful, time seemed insufficient. Yet I felt there would be value in sharing with others events that testify of God's love and faithfulness.

On one occasion I needed to buy medicine for the baby. I drove to the drugstore and sent my 9-year-old son in with my last ten dollars, instructing him to go straight to the pharmacy. After a while, he returned to the car empty handed ... he had lost the money! Regaining my composure, I consoled my tearful son and told him we would pray and trust God to help us. We went back into the store and found the money under a ballglove in the toy section, where he had become distracted. Later, reviewing the incident, I exclaimed, "I should write about this!" But I didn't.

When I became upset about an article in the newspaper, my children heard me declare, "I'm going to write to the editor!" Yet it was much simpler to verbalize frustrations than to put them into words on paper.

Recently my husband died. After caring for him over a span of several months, I realized I had other stories I wanted to write about God's sustaining grace and comfort. Again I thought aloud, "I still want to write someday."

Today I picked up my pen and began writing, as excited thoughts tumbled through my mind.

My "someday" is now "today."

Loving God, thanks for being so patient with me and waiting until my "someday" turned into "today" so I could ...

_____

_____

_____

_____

_____

Irene Van Liew resides in Phoenix, Arizona. She enjoys writing poetry and humorous sketches, and has interest in writing inspirational articles. Irene uses her spiritual gift of encouragement through various avenues in her local church. This devotional is her first published work.

LIGHT ON A HILL

Ruth Vaughn

*Ye are the light of the world...men [put] a candle on a
candlestick; and it giveth light unto all..."*
(Matthew 5:14,15, KJV)

Life hurt me this year.

Self-esteem plummeted. I sat on the muddy bottom
of ocean depths and was devil beaten by the lie-whip
that my life would never surface to shore again. My
"candle" was doused in oceanic forces of defeat beyond
repair.

In the aphotic midnight hour, I wrote in my journal:
"What does it matter if my life-light is darkened in a
hurting world? I, the word-professional book-writing,
lectern-speaking, am no longer valuable. My candle
wax is soaked.

"And...I am so small...yet a candle wick is only a
short string...but its radiance can make the difference
in life-darkness for those whose lives touch my own...be
it en masse as highly visible communicator or be it
one-on-one in the small town where I live alone."

Inner words challenged: "Ruth, I have chosen you."

*Those are your challenge words, aren't they Lord?
You believe in me when I cannot.*

"I have chosen you."

To be what? A self-pitying failure on life's ocean depths? Or to be "the light of the world" that can "so shine before men that they may see your good works, and glorify your Father which is in heaven?"

I am not a candle brand new in perfection from life's mold. I am a "veteran" candle whose light has come through the darkness of thunder, tornado, midnight and gone in the sunshine, splendored daylight of many life seasons.

I am not beautiful or freshly unwrapped from plastic covering. Although scarred from much use, I am still the "light of the world."

True. "I am so small...yet a candle wick is only a short string, but its radiance can make the difference in life-darkness for those whose lives touch my own"

Good Shepherd, You have chosen me to ...

_____

_____

_____

_____

_____

_____

Ruth Vaughn is the author of 39 books including *Write To Discover Yourself* (Doubleday), and a teacher/speaker in tours throughout three nations. She lives in Bethany, Oklahoma.

You are —
the Light of the
World.
A city on a hill cannot
be hidden.
Neither do people light a
lamp and put it under
a bowl.

No, they put it on its stand,
and it gives light to
everyone in the house.

In the same way, let your
Light Shine,

that all people may see your
Good Deeds
and Praise Your Father
in Heaven.

LEIGH KNOWLES

MATTHEW
5:14-16

PRESSING TOWARD THE GOAL

Vivian Vernon

I count not myself yet to have laid hold: but one thing I do, forgetting the things which are behind, and stretching forward to the things which are before, I press on toward the goal unto the prize of the high calling of God in Christ Jesus. (Philippians 3:13-14, KJV)

Sue was absorbed in typing an article. She had researched her material and organized her notes. It was exciting to see her thoughts coming alive on the paper and she didn't even hear the thud as the mail dropped through the door slot. She glanced at her watch. Time for lunch already? She picked up the mail, opening the envelopes as she dashed to the kitchen. Rejection slips again! Laying them on the table, she began making a salad.

Her husband, Jim, came in whistling. He picked up the rejected manuscripts. "Don't you ever get discouraged, Sue?" he asked as he gave her a big hug. "What are you going to do with these now? You've sent them out several times already."

"I'm going to make some improvements and send them off again," Sue answered. "I have a list of publishers I haven't tried. God gave me this talent, Jim,

and He expects me to use it for Him. When I get a
rejection I just remind myself that His Word tells me to
forget the past and keep pressing on toward the goal."

"You pray a lot about your writing, don't you, Sue?
That's why you never give up."

Sue looked solemn. "You're right," she said. "With
my God-given talent and your encouragement I know I
will be a published writer someday."

How about you? Your faith and determination can
make you a successful Christian writer, too.

Gracious Lord Jesus, assist me as I press toward ...

_____

_____

_____

_____

_____

_____

_____

Vivian Vernon, of Mesa, Arizona, began the Christian Writer's club
in nearby Tempe. A minister's wife for 45 years, she has written
and produced plays and puppet shows, taught workshops in drama
and Christian education, and published stories, articles and
devotionals in many magazines. She also speaks at
mother-daughter banquets and women's retreats.

A DREAM— A COMMITMENT

Esther Loewen Vogt

So I was afraid and went out and hid your talent in the
ground...His Master replied, "Take the talent from him
and give it to the one who has the ten talents."
(Matthew 25:24-28, NIV)

I was a child of the Depression and reading
materials were scarce at home. Our little country
school had a surprisingly well-stocked library and I soon
discovered the joys of reading. Yet always I yearned to
write the kind of stories I loved to read.

As a farm girl, the middle of five sisters, I plotted
stories while I helped my father plow the fields and milk
cows. Mom called me "the Dreamer."

In high school and college my English teachers
encouraged me to develop my writing skills. I shrugged
it off. I was just a simple country girl, a nobody.

After my marriage in 1942, I settled down to fulfill
my job as a wife and mother to our three children,
dashing off an occasional ditty or story for

self-expression. One day after reading Matthew 25 I was appalled by the story of the buried talent.

God clearly stepped off the page and shook his finger at me. "Esther, if you don't use your writing talent, you'll lose it."

"Okay, Lord," I cried. "I will — if you provide the opportunities!"

With these words I began a lifetime of writing. Slowly, steadily, my stories began to sell. Now, hundred of short stories and 8 adult and children's books later (mostly fiction), I'm still writing. Books have become my forte, especially historicals.

I discovered that as I committed my writing to Him, the Lord fulfilled my dream of "someday writing the kinds of stories I loved to read." Communicating God's love to others through writing became my service for Him.

Almighty Lord, You have provided the talent. It is up to me to ...

_____

_____

_____

_____

_____

Besides writing **Esther Vogt's** 8 published books, she enjoys leading workshops at writers' conferences on topics such as Writing Historical Fiction, and others. A resident of Hillsboro, Kansas, she is also an instructor for Christian Writers Institute in the Fiction and Writing the Novel courses.

MY FOCUS

Linda R. Wade

And the Lord came and called as before, "Samuel!
Samuel!" And Samuel replied, "Yes, I'm listening."
(1 Samuel 3:10, TLB)

My plane ticket for a Christian Writer's Conference
rested securely in my purse. Family arrangements were
made. Stories and articles were tucked in the attache
case. Then the doubts began. I dreamed of bad
accidents and writing embarrassments. Was this a
forewarning, I asked myself. I prayed and agonized in
the decision to go or stay home.

Finally at 11 P.M. on the night before the
conference, I made my decision. "Dear Lord," I prayed,
"You have opened all the doors for me to go and I'm
stepping out on faith believing that this doubt and
confusion is not coming from You." I told my family
and began to pack the suitcase. My mind cleared and
peace covered me. I slept soundly for the first time in a
week.

From the moment I left Fort Wayne, I knew
something special would happen. And it did. A
speaker spoke on Habakkuk 2:2, "Write the vision, and
make it plain upon tables, that he may run that readeth
it." (KJV) I suddenly realized that God was speaking to
my heart. I remember weeping like a child and
answering as did Samuel. "Speak, Lord, for your
servant is listening."

Then a small voice seemed to say, "Linda, write the vision, write of my love, write my message. Reach out to those who need to be told that God cares." I left the conference with new zeal.

I've never forgotten that afternoon. The focus and the commitment remains the same today. Sometimes it rests on the back burner while more pressing matters are dealt with, but that calling is imprinted on my very being. I must write, even when I don't want to. I must follow where God opens doors even when it means personal sacrifice. My focus challenges me and remains intact!

Even today as I read the story of Samuel and Eli, I put my name in place of Samuel; and I still reply to the call, "Yes, I'm listening."

Lord, I'm listening. Your voice seems to say ...

_____

_____

_____

_____

_____

_____

Linda Wade has written for many devotionals including *Come Ye Apart, Upper Room Disciplines 1983, Table Talk*, and *Quiet Hour*. Two books for children were published in 1989 and a new series of eight books for children were released in 1991, along with four Presidential read-alongs for children. She also is a speaker at writers conferences. She makes her home in Fort Wayne, Indiana.

SURELY NOT ME, LORD!

Shirley Pope Waite

How foolish you are, and how slow of heart to believe.
(Luke 24:25a, NIV)

I've come down with another bad case of the doldrums, and am wailing in self-pity.

Setbacks in my career, nagging physical problems and strained family relationships prompt me to chant that worn-out tune, "Poor me!"

Then I receive a contributor's copy of a devotional booklet.

As every writer knows, there's a gap of weeks, months, perhaps even years when your "masterpiece" finally sees print. I don't know about others, but when my "marked copy" arrives, I may have forgotten what I wrote. In fact, on a couple of occasions, I failed to recognize my own writing.

And then it happens! My own writing ministers back to me!

One of my devotions ends with this prayer: "Father, slow me down. Teach me loving ways to handle frustration."

In another, I mention the unlimited provisions available through our Lord. "Whatever we require," I tell the reader, "we need only come to Him and take what we need from His vast storehouse." And my prayer at the end of that devotion! "Thank you, Lord, that You have exactly what I need, when and where I need it!"

O foolish woman, how slow of heart to believe!

Jesus, thank you for all that I have and for fulfilling my needs, which are ...

_____

_____

_____

_____

_____

_____

_____

_____

_____

_____

Shirley Pope Waite has been published in several books and magazines, teaches at area community colleges, and leads women's retreats. She resides in Walla Walla, Washington.

ISLANDS

Georgiana Walker

*Come away by yourselves to a lonely place and rest a
while.* (Mark 6:31, NAS)

Saturdays my husband and I like to begin the day
with an early morning walk. We have a rule for our
walks: no talking except for conversation about the
things we see. We don't mention leaky faucets, pressing
deadlines, commitments for the coming week, bills to be
paid, or any such thing. We close the door on our
chores and challenges and head for the nearby park.

As we prowl the park's paths and roads, we enjoy
the squirrels, the rabbits, and trees. We watch for birds
and listen to their different sounds and songs. We talk
about the foothills stretching to the north and wonder
what animals live there. One morning we saw two
coyotes. Another time a deer startled us as it dashed
across our path.

Before we start home we usually sit for a while on
steps near the fountain. We are quiet. We thank God
for the wonders of His creation that surround us. We
praise Him for His greatness. We pray for strength and
wisdom for the day ahead.

George and I call these morning walks our "islands"
-- quiet, restful spots we create in the ebb and flow of
our busy lives.

If there are mornings we can't get away, we have
discovered that even an hour late in the evening can be
a restful "island." Last night George read to me for
awhile. Then we sat on the front porch steps listening
to night sounds and counting stars.

The day Jesus said to his disciples, "Come...rest a while," they had been so busy they hadn't even taken time to eat.

Does that sound familiar? If you feel burned out from your writing, and a schedule packed full of commitments, "Come...rest a while." Create some quiet "islands" for yourself. And in the quietness reach out to God for strength and wisdom for the days ahead.

Creator Father, You have created all things. I know it's up to me to explore ...

_____

_____

_____

_____

_____

_____

_____

_____

Georgiana Walker, now retired, was an editor/writer at Gospel Light Publications as well as a frequent faculty member at various writers conferences. From her home in Glendale, California, she continues to edit and write on assignment and teaches an adult Bible class. Her current project is putting together a family history for the Walkers' thirteen grandchildren.

WRITING CAN'T WAIT

Barbara Leonard Warren

This day will I begin to magnify thee.
(Joshua 3:7, KJV)

I need some help, Lord — right this minute! After all, You said, "Ask, and it shall be given you" (Luke 11:9) and I'm asking. Begging, actually.

Why am I so scared to sit down at my typewriter today? All I have to do is walk across the room, pull out my chair, sit down and start to write. Write — yes, that's the problem today. What if I can't think of anything to write? Or, if I manage to think of something, what if I can't put it into words?

Maybe I should scrub the bathtub first. I haven't vacuumed the living room carpet this week either. Perhaps I should bake a few loaves of bread. The yeasty cooking odors might inspire me to write.

Help, Lord! When household chores sound better than writing, I really do have a problem. Yes, I know I can write. At least, I could write last week. But perhaps I've forgotten how. Where are You when I need You, Lord? I'm asking. I'm begging.

I tell friends I like to write. That's why I often get up at 5 A.M. on weekdays and write for an hour before leaving for my teaching job. That's why I spend weekend and vacations writing and rewriting.

I do want to write. It's getting started that's so hard. But I want to share Your Word with others, Lord. The bathtub can wait; the closet can wait; the bread can wait. Your work can't wait. I'm going to walk over to my typewriter and begin writing. Now.

Lord Jesus, this day I will begin to ...

_____

_____

_____

_____

_____

_____

_____

_____

Barbara Leonard Warren is president of Imagine Rainbows, Inc., which features writing, speaking, photography and other forms of communication. A resident of Arizona City, Arizona, she is the publisher and author of two books and former women's editor of the *Prescott Courier*. She has also written hundreds of newspaper and magazines articles, and is a member of MENSA's Gifted Children's Speakers' Bureau.

I BRAKE FOR WRITERS

James Watkins

Looking unto Jesus the author and finisher of our faith.
(Hebrews 12:2, KJV)

Computer printers make me nervous. My stomach feels as if it, too, is being fed through the roller. My heart keeps rhythm with the 500-words-per-minute percussion of the print wheel. My eyes track the newly formed letters as my thoughts of the moment are permanently pounded onto paper. A few weeks later 50,000 copies will be printed. By the time complimentary copies arrive, I won't be satisfied with what I have written. And that's what scares me.

But I'm not alone. Andy Rooney wonders, "How come what I wrote last year, last month, last week and even yesterday, doesn't seem quite right?"

There is something, however, that I fear even more: that someday I might be satisfied with what I wrote a month ago. That would mean I would have ceased to mature mentally or spiritually for 30 days! Howard Hendricks has put it well: "When we stop growing, we start dying." That's why you'll never read *The Completed Works of James N. Watkins* -- at least while I'm still living!

Obviously, God's Truth will never change. But our knowledge, comprehension, and application of it must continue to grow until we receive that big royalty check in the sky.

Thus, our attitudes, values, priorities, perspectives and relationships need to be constantly revised.

Books and articles, then, are never "final copy." Whatever draft a writer is working on when the publisher calls, is the collection of thoughts that is typeset, printed, bound, and shipped off to bookstores as "truth."

Perhaps the computer age will allow for electronic books — and take-home papers — that can be constantly revised. For this is what "the author and finisher of our faith" wants us to be doing until we reach "the measure of all the fullness of God."

Father, I feel Your presence saying its time to update ...

_____

_____

_____

_____

_____

_____

James Watkins is the author of nine books and over six hundred articles. He speaks at several writer's conferences each year and resides in LaOtto, Indiana.

LETTER TO CHRIST

C. Ellen Watts

*You show that you are a letter from Christ...written not
with ink but with the Spirit of the living God, not on
tablets of stone but on tablets of human hearts.*

(2 Corinthians 3:3, NIV)

"The story idea is great. Your best yet.
Unfortunately..."

A fly buzzed between kitchen window and screen,
then dropped to the sill. As the editor's message
registered, I felt like that fly — caught between a
hard-nosed editorial committee and my own feelings of
inadequacy.

I thanked the editor for calling and crept to my
favorite corner of the sofa. Where I live, it was barely
7 A.M.— too early in the morning to be told that ten
dreamed-for writing projects had been reduced to two.
While twenty years of free-lancing had taught me that
rejection can strike often and in any day's mail, I
wanted to howl out loud.

Murmuring something like, "Lord, why!" I scrubbed
away tears, picked up the Bible I'd laid aside and
resumed my studies in Paul's second letter to the
Corinthians, chapter three.

I blinked at verse two. "You yourselves are our letter...known and read by everybody."

Verse three insisted my ministry was written with the Spirit of the Living God and not with my word processor as I had supposed. My neat words on long grain 20 pound bond were hardly synonyms for daily Christlike living.

How dear of God to affirm during my disappointment that I am His letter from Christ. An assignment, large or small, scarcely compares to the manner in which I live my life today.

What I write and what is published, however, should bear testimony to the Spirit of the living God who lives within my heart because it is through writing that my ministry is extended.

Heavenly Father, I need Your comfort today because ...

_____

_____

_____

_____

_____

_____

_____

C. Ellen Watts of Nampa, Idaho, authored a missionary biography, two young adult novels, *It Can't Happen to Me* and *Moving Again! I'm Not Going*; and hundreds of short stories and articles for the take-home market. She also conducts frequent writing seminars.

PROGRAMMED

FOR

WRITING

Dorothy Wells

I press toward the mark for the prize of the high calling of God in Christ Jesus. (Philippians 3:14, KJV)

In my profession as a nurse, a "care plan" is a vital tool in the assessment and implementation of patient care. This plan gives direction to the medical team for the positive outcome to the patient.

There are "care plans" in other fields as well. Architects use a blueprint. Engineers use a schematic drawing.

Writers also need a plan. An inspirational idea comes and we jot it down on a scrap of paper and stuff it in a drawer. But without a plan it will remain there. It takes effort to share our experiences with others. We need to set goals, both short and long term, and push toward these goals. Sometimes it takes a deadline to motivate us.

Paul stated, "I press toward the mark." Before his conversion, he was ambitious to persecute Christians. After a dramatic encounter with Jesus, he found a new goal — to fulfil God's purpose in his life. As he stretched to the limit to grasp the prize, he gave us a vivid example of a goal setter.

Jesus said the builder of a house should plan it well. As Christian writers, we need to define our goals and set out determined to reach them.

God, I set before You this plan of action ...

_____

_____

_____

_____

_____

_____

_____

_____

_____

_____

_____

Dorothy Wells, of Cottonwood, Arizona, writes for her church newsletter, has been published in *The Upper Room*, and enjoys writing inspirational articles. She is completing 40 years of active nursing.

$\mathcal{A}$
$\mathcal{ROYAL}$
$\mathcal{POSITION}$

Bonnie G. Wheeler

And who knows but that you have come to royal position
for such a time as this? (Esther 4:14, KJV)

When I first signed my book contract I felt confident that I could approach the subject with the professional objectivity of a researcher/writer.

As I started interviewing and researching, painful scenes from my childhood started surfacing. The opposition I felt and the long buried memories seemed more than I could deal with.

"Hey, Lord...I'm not really qualified for this project, maybe you should get someone else for this. Lord...this hurts too much and I want out!"

At a timely conference, the keynote speaker was talking about Queen Esther and read the verse, "And who knows but that you have come to royal position for such a time as this?"

Suddenly the pieces started coming together. I had arrived not to "royal" position, but to a certain place as a writer where I was asked to tackle a timely topic. The painful memories took on new meaning. Through my writing, God could take my private pain and use it for public healing.

With renewed commitment I sat down at my typewriter, "For such a time as this..."

Dear Lord, for such a time as this ...

_____

_____

_____

_____

_____

_____

_____

_____

_____

_____

_____

Bonnie Wheeler, of Hayward, California, is a speaker, author of three books: *Of Braces and Blessings, Challenged Parenting,* and *The Hurrier I Go*, contributing author to 12 other books, and writer of over 200 articles. She speaks at conferences on such subjects as disabilities, time management and writing.

BACK TO LYSTRA

Esther Wilkison

Therefore, my beloved brethren, be ye steadfast, unmovable, always abounding in the work of the Lord, forasmuch as ye know that your labor is not in vain in the Lord. (I Corinthians 15:58, KJV)

A bulletin board hung in the staff lounge at a camp where I counseled one summer. Pinned to the board was the activity schedule, a menu, a few yellowed comic strips, and a reminder from the Program Director about keeping the archery equipment put away. I remember at some point in the summer someone pinned up a note on a half sheet of notebook paper. Carefully printed with a Magic Marker were the words:

> To avoid criticism:
> say nothing
> do nothing
> be nothing

At times I fear I'm dreadfully close to the "be nothing" stage. After pouring my heart out to the teens I teach and coach, it hurts to hear criticism.

Anyone in leadership tries to communicate a message. That message, or the motive behind it, may be misunderstood. So the criticism comes, often bringing waves of disillusionment and discouragement in its tide.

The Apostle Paul was rejected. After preaching God's loving message of hope to the people at Lystra, they didn't applaud. They didn't send him loving notes of affirmation. They stoned him. They didn't want him or his message. Paul didn't decide to "be nothing" to avoid all the pain and frustration. He went back to Lystra. (Acts 14:19-21)

I have my own Lystra. Perhaps we all do.

Father in heaven, I pray that You don't allow criticism to block my path. Instead, let me use ...

_____

_____

_____

_____

_____

_____

_____

_____

Esther Wilkison teaches sixth graders at a Phoenix, Arizona school where she also coaches volleyball, basketball, and elementary cheerleading. Esther writes poetry, has been published in an Evergreen devotional book, and has a juvenile novel in process.

COMFORT IN TIME OF NEED

Anne Williman

*He comforts us in all our troubles, so that we in turn may
be able to comfort others.*   (2 Corinthians 1:4a, NEB)

It had not been a good day. The children bickered,
the dog threw up on the rug, and I was discouraged by
some overwhelming problems about which I'd been
praying for years. Yet nothing had changed. Where
was God?

After lunch, my pre-schooler went down for a nap.
With my older child playing quietly in her room, I
collapsed with the mail.

Tossing aside the rejections for later, I tore open an
envelope of contributor's copies. Not as good as a sale,
but maybe it would help.

I began reading my article. And something strange
happened. It was as if I'd never read the words. I was
struck by the uncomplicated story of a person in need
and how God answered her prayer.

How had I forgotten that incident? I thought about
other personal experience pieces I'd written —
examples of God's faithfulness to me. Then it hit me:
The Lord had been there for me then; wouldn't He also
be here at this time? It was so simple, but how I

needed that message at that moment.

I asked the Lord's forgiveness for my lack of faith. Then I thanked Him for using my own article to remind me that He was still taking care of things in my life.

One of my main goals in my writing is to use the painful times I've been through — and God's provision during them — to comfort others in hurting places. But I realized that day — sometimes the one who needs that ministry the most is me.

Beloved Father, who provides comfort always, let me remember ...

_____

_____

_____

_____

_____

_____

_____

The author of three books, **Anne Williman** has had over 350 sales to Christian magazines. Her newest book, *Mary of Magdala*, a Biblical novel published by Broadman, was a featured main selection for Family Bookshelf Book Club. Ann lives in Old Fort, Ohio.

WRITE ABOUT HIM

Sherwood Wirt

Except the Lord build the house, they labor in vain that build it. (Psalm 127:1, KJV)

Several years ago, before the computer age, while editor at *Decision* magazine, I paraphrased the above Psalm for myself: "Except the Lord keep the copy, the typewriter clacketh in vain."

Since then I have graduated to a word processor, but the principle holds. I spent a quarter of a century baffled by a block — not the kind that grips and paralyzes a writer's mind, but the sheer frustration of writing books that no one wanted to publish. When the breakthrough finally came, it was as if the skies opened and a personal message came down from heaven: "Write about Me and your obstructions will disappear."

My first book was about the Beatitudes. It led to another book, then another. Again and again the message was driven home: "People don't want to read about you. They want to read about Me. Write about My Word. Make it come alive. Bring it to your generation. Leave the rest to Me."

The biggest writer's block, I believe, is discouragement. After teaching in writer's conferences around the world, I have encountered many victims of disappointment; the rejection slips roll in and the lights go out. But when I open my Bible and begin to go over the old familiar promises, I find myself thinking, "I'd like to share that. I'd like to tell people what that passage means, and what it can do for them. That's great. That's what we need. Where's a pencil?"

My Lord and Savior, as You direct my thoughts, let me ...

_____

_____

_____

_____

_____

_____

_____

_____

_____

Sherwood Wirt is best known as the founder of *Decision* magazine where he served as editor for 16 years. A resident of Poway, California, he is the author of 23 books, including his latest, a novel entitled *The Doomsday Connection*. In 1977, Dr. Wirt founded the San Diego County Christian Writers' Guild which now has 250 members.

Bless the Lord

oh my soul;
and all that
is within me,,

Bless

HIS HOLY NAME

© LEIGH KNOWLES

PSALM 103-1

LORD, ESTABLISH THE WORK OF OUR HANDS

Nancy Witmer

May the favor of the Lord our God rest upon us; establish the work of our hands for us — yes, establish the work of our hands. (Psalm 90:17, NIV)

I'm quitting," I said, dumping a stack of returned manuscripts in the lap of a writer friend. "I can't take this rejection."

Instead of commiserating with me, my friend read the above verse, "I don't think you should give up yet," she said. "The Lord is going to establish the work of your hands — your writing."

In the years since that conversation, this verse has comforted me when my mailbox yielded pregnant SASEs instead of slim acceptance letters and checks. Or when a hoped-for assignment went to another writer. Since I believe that God was establishing the work of my hands, I could relax. I didn't need to scheme, or push, or compete in order to grasp success for myself.

On the other hand, I didn't just sit back and expect God to hand me success in a neat package. I've worked hard to improve my writing skills by independent study and by attending writer's conferences and seminars.

As you and I stretch to achieve our goals as Christian writers, let us do so knowing that God is the One Who establishes our work. As we continue to pursue excellence in our craft, we can rest in the fact that our success comes from the Lord.

Loving God, don't allow me to quit, but send an angel to remind me of Your promises so that I may ...

_____

_____

_____

_____

_____

_____

_____

Nancy Witmer began free-lancing in 1982 and has been published more than 350 times in 50 different publications. In 1990, she received an AMY Writing Award. She lives in Manheim, Pennsylvania.

PREREQUISITE TO WRITING

O. Dell Woods

*In the beginning was the Word, and the Word was with
God, and the Word was God.* (John 1:1, NIV)

Our creative writing class broke into laughter as the
instructor told about a man who wanted to be a writer.
The reason: he'd heard writers make lots of money,
they don't have to keep regular hours and they get to
appear on TV shows.

Before launching our writing careers, many of us
hold that view. Once we begin, though, we find we
must commit to reading, researching, outlining,
marketing and many other non-glamorous tasks before
we ever enter the first word into our word processors.
At that point, we sometimes wish we had taken up
corporate law instead.

Christian writers have another prerequisite to
writing. To prepare our hearts for ministry, we begin
reading God's Word — the Bible, and listening through
prayer to the living Word — Jesus Christ.

Most of us won't make "lots of money" and we may
never appear with Sally or Oprah. We may even find
we have to keep regular hours. However, we can be
successful as Christian writers when we are dedicated to

the Lord and committed to our craft.

Almighty God, I want to dedicate to You ...

O. Dell Woods, a creative Bible teacher and Christian writer from Yarnell, Arizona, writes a newspaper column, "Ona's Potpourri," for *The Traveler.*

FRIENDS

Woody Young

There is a friend who sticks closer than a brother.
(Proverbs 18:24, KJV)
Let your light so shine before men, that they may see your good works, and glorify your Father, who is in Heaven.
(Matthew 5:15, KJV)

Are you like me when you make a new friend? Do you want to know more about that person? And does it seem the more you know about your friend's personal feelings, the closer emotionally you become to each other. Some friends are so close you can identify traits each has picked up from the other.

Friends are open, vulnerable, sincere, inseparable, truthful. And they know each other so well that, emotionally, they know exactly how the other one feels. That's how I feel about my friend, Jesus Christ.

For most of my life, I considered Jesus my Master, the King of my life. He was abstract, a concept, but not truly a personal Friend. However, since I have started to look at Him as not only my Lord and Savior, but also my Friend, I can't seem to stop wanting to know more about Him.

Therefore, if I could pass on anything to others who read my writings or listen to my talks, it would be the friendship of Jesus Christ. For you who have that type of a relationship, you know what I am talking about. And to you who aren't quite sure, I encourage you to start today, by asking Jesus to be your personal Friend, and then start treating Him as the closest and most intimate Friend you have.

And you know what? The highest compliment you can receive is when readers or listeners share how you have started to reflect the traits of your close Friend, Jesus, and, more importantly, how you have helped them into a new relationship with Him.

Gracious Lord Jesus, please be my ...

_____

_____

_____

_____

_____

_____

_____

_____

_____

Woody Young, author (or co-author) of 17 books, speaker, business executive, and publisher, lives with his wife and two daughters in Fountain Valley, California. He is the founder and President of Joy Publishing (which was awarded Small Press Publisher of the Year in 1991) and speaks frequently at writer's conferences.

Epilogue

Now that you've finished this book, we'd like to hear from you.

We hope, and pray, that this collection of devotionals has ministered to you in an extra special way. Please let us know how the Lord has spoken to you through your reading of it.

Your correspondence will encourage and inspire the 100 plus fellow Christians who have shared part of themselves with you through their writings.

Woody Young
c/o Joy Publishing
P.O. Box 827-MM
San Juan Capistrano CA 92675

Prayers ...

Order Form

To order additional copies of this book, you may either:

1. Contact any of the authors and request ordering information from them. OR

2. Contact your local Christian bookstore. OR

3. Send $9.95 (plus $1.95 for shipping and handling) to
Joy Publishing
P.O. Box 827-MM
San Juan Capistrano CA 92675

Please send me _____ copies of
100 Plus Motivational Moments for Writers and Speakers

I am enclosing $11.90 ($9.95 book price, $1.95 shipping/handling) for each copy ordered.

Please send my book(s) to:

Name _____

Address _____

City/State/Zip _____

Phone _____

Other books by Joy Publishing:

A business guide to **Copyright Law**
What You Don't Know Can Co$t You!
by Woody Young $14.95
An easy to understand guide with all necessary forms.

Christian Writers Market Guide
by Sally E. Stuart $18.95
Info. on publishers & editors addresses & phone # plus hints

100+ Party Games
by Sally E. Stuart and Woody Young $7.95
Wholesome games for all ages & group sizes

100+ Craft & Gift Ideas
by Sally E. Stuart and Woody Young $9.95
Fun & easy ideas for parties & holidays

Secrets of Life Every Teen Needs to Know
Dr. Terry Paulson and Sean Paulson$6.95
Favorite family lectures written for teens

write His answer
by Marlene Bagnull $6.95
Devotionals that minister to writers

So You've Been Asked To Pray
by Dr. John B. Toay and Woody Young $9.95
Thoughts for the day and Invocations for all occasions

Poetry Readings at the Panama Hotel
by Denella Kimura $6.95